GENERAL PRINCIPLES OF PLAY
DIRECTION

The Pasadena Community Playhouse

GENERAL PRINCIPLES

OF

PLAY DIRECTION

BY

GILMOR BROWN

AND

ALICE GARWOOD

SAMUEL FRENCH

NEW YORK   LOS ANGELES

SAMUEL FRENCH Ltd. LONDON

PN
2053
B7

CONTENTS

GENERAL PRINCIPLES OF PLAY
DIRECTION

GENERAL PRINCIPLES OF PLAY DIRECTION

CHAPTER I

THE DIRECTOR'S MEDIA

The Director as an Interpretive Artist. The director of a play is an interpretive artist. He takes the script, which is a dead thing that can live only in the imagination of those who read it, and he brings it to life on the stage. The actors help in this vivification, but it is the director whose imagination conceives just what form that life must take. The actors can only create within that form. The greater the amount of vivid life a director can obtain by letting his imagination play around the script, the greater his stature as an artist.

No matter how vivid an imagination a man may have he only becomes an artist when he can give that imagination expression. To give expression to his idea, to create something beautiful, the artist must have a technical mastery of the materials with which he works. The greater the mastery the more nearly will the finished work of art conform to the artist's inspiration.

This book considers the media with which the director works and the laws governing their use.

There are three essential elements which the director uses in interpreting a play. They are the actor, the stage and light.

Settings and costumes are assets, the use of which the director in the modern theatre will do well to understand thoroughly for they are elements that may greatly enhance the emotional values of the play. Unwisely used, however, they may be equally detractive. It is more effective to give a play without scenery and without costumes than to allow those elements to usurp attention that should not be theirs. In the great periods of the past, the Elizabethan theatre used no setting, the Greek theatre, a conventional one. Such costumes as were used were largely the clothes of the period. From the point of view of the director's media the setting may be considered as part of the stage, the costumes as part of the actors.

Light. Light differs from settings and costumes, because it is an essential element of production at least as far as it is used for the purposes of visibility. In a "radio drama" the actors are heard but not seen. It may be good entertainment, it may even be art, but it is certainly not theatre. Before the invention of illuminating gas, visibility was the sole function of light in the theatre. It had no dramatic use. With the power to control light, to govern its intensity and color, it rapidly became a more and more powerful means of arousing emotional response in the audience. The use of light for this purpose is too large a subject to be discussed in detail in this book on play direction, but the director who does not understand and use this element as a vital part of his production is neglecting a powerful factor in securing the dramatic effects he wishes to obtain. There are many excellent books published on the subject. We will discuss it in this one only incidentally as it modifies or changes the use of other elements used in production.

The Stage. The stage or playing space must have the power to attract and hold the attention of the audience. Any type of playing space which has that essential quality may serve as a stage, but its arrangement and limits are imposed by that necessity. In motion pictures the recording apparatus, which represents the attention of the audience, is mobile and this mobility makes it possible to use an almost unlimited playing area. Motion picture scenarios are prepared with this in mind. Plays, however, written for the theatre, are planned for a limited playing space.

The physical laws of light that govern visibility, and, to a certain extent those of sound that govern audibility, limit the type of playing space that it is possible to use. A play given on the same level with the audience could not be seen, but an audience, seated on the level, can still see a stage raised sufficiently above them. A banked audience can see a stage set below their level. In most modern theatres a combination of both the banked audience and the platform is used, and the combination has proved satisfactory in supplying a playing space that is visible to audiences of almost any size.

Ludwig Lewisohn has referred to the stage as "this

mechanism which stripped to its essential is but a wooden platform sheltered from the winds, this simple thing placed now on a hillside, now in an inn-yard, now in a room"—and certainly the "wooden platform" is the mechanism the theatre has used generally throughout its history to catch and hold the attention of the audience. As Lewisohn further says, "From a platform you cannot speak to one man; you speak to many."

The tendency of modern thought in the theatre is toward a playing space of greater intimacy than that afforded by the platform, especially the platform set behind a proscenium arch. There have been many stages designed recently that abolish the arch and curtain and, in many instances, that eliminate any architectural division between the audience and the playing space except that of the raised level used for the stage. Such theatres do retain the platform in its essentials though it may be broken into a series of levels by the use of steps, ramps and platforms leading up from the audience level.

Attempts to create even greater intimacy by eliminating the platform have taken various forms, the two most common being the small studio type theatre, with informal acting areas varying from production to production, and the arena theatre, with the audience banked on all sides of the playing space.

The essential need for focusing the attention of the audience on the playing space means that it must be distinct and different from the space allotted to the audience. In the studio theatre light and its absence perform the functions of the platform and curtain in the ordinary playhouse. That such an arrangement is more conducive to intimacy is undoubted but it is not practical for use except in a theatre designed for a very small audience.

In an arena theatre the playing space is more definitely separated from the audience, at least as to level, so that visibility is not a problem no matter what the size of the audience. The fact that the action takes place in the midst of the audience does create a feeling of closer relationship between actors and audience. The amount of intimacy attained, however, will vary inversely with the increase in size of the auditorium, just as it does in the ordinary platform theatre.

What any type of playing space, having the audience on more than one side, gains in intimacy it will lose in uniformity of impression. When the audience sits on only one side of the playing space the various acting areas on the stage have approximately the same attention-value for each member of the audience. The actor's playing positions, that is full face to audience, in profile, back to audience and the intermediate positions, will be the same for the entire audience. On a stage surrounded by the audience, each playing area will have, unless some other factor is introduced, a different value for different sections of the audience. It will be closer to some and further from others. The playing areas on such a stage may be given a more or less uniform value by the use of levels or, when it is artificially illuminated, by varying the intensity of light on the different areas. The actor's playing positions, however, have of necessity a different value for the various sections of the audience. If he stands facing some he will have his back to others.

The director's use of these elements will be discussed fully in later chapters, largely from the point of view of the platform stage, since that is the equipment with which present day directors usually have to work. The general principles governing the director's use of acting areas and playing positions of his actors can by some modification and adapting be applied to any type of stage.

Every medium of artistic expression has its limitations. It is those limitations that give it its peculiar suitability for the creation of a definite work of art and the closer the conformation between the idea and the medium the greater the integrity and beauty of that work of art. A Beethoven symphony was written for an orchestra not a brass band. A play is written for production on a stage, that is in a playing space with definite limits and qualities. The limits and qualities of the playing space at the director's command will determine the type of play that he produces and the director's technique, as far as the stage is concerned, consists of using his playing space as an artistic medium, of making its limitations and qualities serve to vivify the play that he is producing.

Actors. Plays may be presented, though not, perhaps, in the theatre, without light and without a stage, but only Gordon Craig has been able to conceive of a play without actors, and even he had to substitute puppets. The actor, therefore, is the most important element with which the director works. It is only in relation to him that the other elements take on value.

Other artists work in inanimate media, pigments, marble, words or sound, media that obey certain set and definite laws, but the director's medium is human beings, each of which is more or less a law unto himself. Each actor is different from all other actors, different in his capabilities both physical and imaginative, and each one varies in his own capabilities from time to time. The director is constantly being surprised by the unexpected qualities and limitations that develop even in an actor that he knows well. It is just the unexpected nature of this medium that makes directing so stimulating.

Moreover the actor is an artist in his own right, a fact that the director should not overlook. The director who insists that his actors interpret their parts and read their lines exactly as he would do it, usually makes a production that is lacking in vitality and spontaneity. Even if the director has real genius as an interpretive artist his productions will tend to have a sameness, just as we say of an actor that he always plays himself. In both cases they fail as artists to take full advantage of all the possibilities of their media. The director must, as an interpretive artist, see that each character as presented by the actor takes on the relationship to the play as a whole that will best serve the director's interpretation of the play, but within those limits the actor should be free to create his own part. The sensitive director, working with a fine actor, will often receive as much inspiration from the actor as the actor receives from the director.

CHAPTER II

THE DIRECTOR'S USE OF THE STAGE

The director's use of the stage as an artistic medium depends on his understanding of the attention-value of its various areas. The six arbitrary areas into which any empty stage, no matter what its size, may be divided, vary in value according to their power to attract and hold attention. These arbitrary areas may be changed in value by the arrangement of the set and lights. The actual playing areas will depend on the furniture arrangement, the placing of doors, windows, fireplaces, etc. They may or may not coincide with the arbitrary areas.

ARBITRARY AREAS

The accompanying diagram shows the division of the stage into the six arbitrary areas.

They are in the order of their attention-value, Down Center, Up Center, Down Right, Down Left, Up Right, and Up Left.

The director's use of right and left should always be from the point of view of the actor. This practice makes it easier for the actor to receive verbal direction during rehearsal. The terms up and down refer to the distance from the audience, up stage being farther away from and down stage closer to the curtain line.

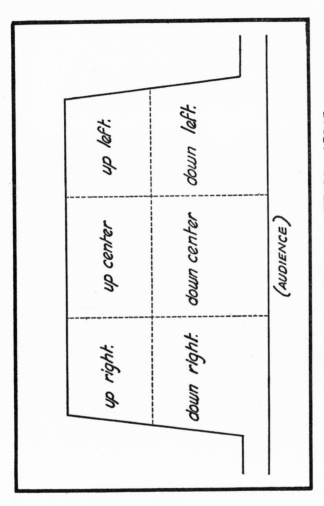

DIAGRAM I – ARBITRARY STAGE AREAS.

9

The terms we will use to denote the relative values of different areas are "strong" and "weak." A strong area is one which has great attention-value, a weak area is one which has little attention-value. These terms are by no means synonymous with good and bad, effective and ineffective or definite and indefinite. Weak areas are used definitely for their qualities just as strong ones are.

The strength and weakness of stage areas are relative. A scene between two actors alone on the stage will take and hold attention even though played in a weak area. If other characters are present in the strong areas the attention of the audience is likely to shift to them unless some other element is present that counteracts the arbitrary strength and weakness of the areas.

A platform or higher level in a weak area will strengthen that area. A more brightly lighted area is strong regardless of its arbitrary value. The focus of other actors may strengthen a scene played in a weak area and the amount of attention an actor receives may depend as much or more on his playing position than on the area in which he stands.

Playing Areas

There may be any number of playing areas on a stage, depending on its size, the design and shape of the set, the position of entrances, the arrangement of furniture, and the use of platforms, steps, etc. These elements may be so arranged as to weaken an arbitrarily strong area or strengthen an arbitrarily weak one. For example, placing a large table down center will weaken the arbitrarily strong up center area by lessening its attention-value. Putting a chair on a platform or dais up right will provide a strong playing area in what is an arbitrarily weak area because the higher level increases the attention-value. Unless there is some good and definite reason for another arrangement, the director should try to make the strength and weakness of the arbitrary areas coincide with and reinforce the strength and weakness that he desires in his playing areas.

Since the arrangement of playing areas is an important element in directing a play it should be planned by the director himself and not left to the scenic artist. Neither need the director comply with the arrangement specified by the playwright. His stage may make deviation necessary or he may feel that by a rearrangement he can better secure the effects he wishes to obtain from the various scenes.

The director will plan the arrangement of furniture, doors, windows, fireplace, etc. to afford the acting areas he desires, to facilitate movement and to motivate business. A natural arrangement is desirable for a realistic play, but, because the stage is art and not nature, such an arrangement may be slightly opened up to give the actors desirable playing positions. If such an opening up is obvious, however, the effect is apt to become artificial. The positions of windows and fireplaces can often be used as a motivation for placing furniture in the desired position. The use of a too stereotyped or conventional stage arrangement of furniture is also apt to create the feeling of artificiality, even though, in itself, it is natural enough.

At least three pieces or groups of furniture are desirable. Each one will be a separate area. If a group is used as one area the pieces should be closely related, as for example two chairs with a small table between them, or a table with chairs about it. It is desirable for each acting area to give opportunity for the seating or relaxed positions of at least two people. A large arm chair can be so used by having the second person sit on the arm; a high back chair by having the second person lean on the back. Acting areas should not all be on the same level, that is equally distant from the curtain line. Some should be farther up stage than others. They should not be too close together or else they lose their values as distinct areas. Enough room should be left between them for easy movement about the stage. If your stage is very small it is better to eliminate the third area than to have the furniture groups too close together.

In planning his acting areas the director must give some consideration to light. Light is an important element in determining the value of playing areas. Furniture grouped near a window in a daytime scene or around a lamp or other light source in an evening scene will afford a strong playing area. Conversely, the director who plans to strengthen a playing area by the use of light should, if his play is realistic, indicate the source of the brighter illumination.

Variety. In a play of more than one set, the director

should plan for variety in the furniture arrangement of the different scenes. It is sometimes possible to get a desirable variety in a one set production by having at least some of the furniture changed about for the different acts. The director who is producing a series of plays for more or less the same audience has the problem of securing variety not only in the settings for the individual plays, but in those used throughout the series.

The Use of Playing Areas. Before going into rehearsal it is advisable for the director to plan his use of playing areas and to know pretty definitely in what areas he wants the various scenes played. The following suggestion should be kept in mind.

1. Avoid using the entire stage except for occasional scenes, preferably those in which a large group of actors are employed, but use at one time or another every area and all the furniture. (Unnecessary or unused furniture is apt to be distracting, especially if the pieces are important or interesting. You can get the atmosphere desired by a careful selection of the needed furniture and by decoration. In the case of a very large stage it may be necessary to use unneeded furniture as trim in order to keep the set from appearing bare. In such a case try to select furniture that will not call attention to itself.)

2. Play an intimate scene between a small number of characters in one area. If only two or three people are on the stage placing them in different areas is apt to create a feeling of indifference or estrangement.

3. Use of the full stage alternating with scenes played in a single area will give emphasis to both scenes by contrast.

4. The use of the same area over and over becomes monotonous. If, however, you have scenes in which the same idea is expressed by contrasting groups of characters it is often effective to play them in the same area and, if you can do so without being obvious, using the same playing positions for the actors. In the same way scenes of strong dramatic contrast may be sharpened and emphasized by being played in the same area. For example: A young man is shown in a scene at the opening of a play returning to his home in triumph. He sits in a certain chair while his devoted mother and sisters wait on him. He receives the admiration and plaudits of friends and neighbors. At the close of the play he is shown broken and deserted. The contrast of the two scenes will be intensified, because the minds of the audience will be led back to the opening scene, if the same chair is used in both.

5. It is sometimes necessary or desirable to use the same area frequently, for emphasis of dramatic values as noted above, because business indicated by the plot demands it, or from lack of space on a small stage. In such a case special attention should be paid to the breaking up within the area, that is to varying the positions of the actors. Sometimes even slight changes of bodily positions will be sufficient to relieve the monotony caused by repeated use of the same area.

6. In trying to avoid monotony in the use of playing areas avoid shifting from one area to another and back again for that in turn becomes monotonous. This is the reason it is desirable to have three acting areas at least. The number of area sequences can be greatly in-

creased if three areas are available. If, however, only two areas are available the monotony may be broken either by standing scenes, or by the use of the stage as a whole. Another element that may create monotony in the use of playing areas is the playing of scenes at the same distance from the curtain line. It is as advisable to vary the playing of your scenes between down stage and up stage as it is to vary them between right and left.

7. In planning the use of playing areas it is often possible to reserve certain areas for certain characters or for certain ideas, so that they become subconsciously associated in the minds of the audience with the characters or ideas. Such an association will often help to heighten the dramatic effect of the scene. It is not usually possible to use more than one area in this symbolic manner during a play, and care must be taken that the symbolism does not become obvious. When the director plans such a use for a given area it should be pointed early in the play, before its actual use as a symbol. That is, another character or other characters should use it. If the character who points the area is also closely associated with the idea for which the main character stands, the pointing is more effective. Suppose, for instance, the play deals with an elderly woman who has met with financial reverses. Rather than face life under the new circumstances she has let herself become a semi-invalid. A large easy chair is reserved as her area by the director. In the first act of the play, before we have seen the invalid, her daughter on whom the burden of financial support has fallen, enters. Tired and discouraged, she throws herself into the easy chair and expresses her

desire to give up the fight. During the scene, however, her courage is regained. First she sits erect in the chair, then forward on its edge, then rises and stands beside it but still close, and when her courage has entirely returned and she is no longer in her mother's habitual state of mind, she moves away.

CHAPTER III

MOVEMENT

Whatever the actor does on the stage, as distinct from what he says, is known in theatre terminology as "business." Business may include anything from crossing the stage to lighting a match. For purposes of clarity, however, we have divided the consideration of what an actor does on the stage into two sections. Any actual change of bodily position, crossing the stage, rising, sitting, etc. we will consider as *Movement;* the term *Business* we will use to cover detailed pantomimic action. The two are very closely related but there is a distinction in the purposes for which a director uses them.

INHERENT AND IMPOSED MOVEMENT

There are two kinds of movement which will appear in every production. Inherent movement is such movement as the story makes necessary. The plot of the play depends on it and the story could not go forward if it were omitted. Imposed movement on the other hand is movement inserted for some technical purpose, to create an effect, desirable for dramatic reasons, but not necessary to the story.

Inherent Movement. Inherent movement, since it is

part of the story, is imagined and specified by the play-wright. It will be found in the stage directions, though not all stage directions are concerned with inherent movement. The playwright may specify imposed move-ment in the stage directions where he feels it to be de-sirable. Inherent movement must be accepted and used by the director. He may vary or change it somewhat to suit his own stage and setting or to make it conform more closely to his interpretation of the play, but he cannot omit it without effecting the story of the play.

Imposed Movement. Imposed movement may, as we have seen, be indicated by the playwright, or it may be invented by the director or the actor. The director does not need to accept the playwright's suggestion, if he feels that such movement is better omitted or changed. His is the final decision on any question of im-posed movement and it usually rests largely with him to decide when any imposed movement is to occur and what it is to be. Imposed movement may be used for any of the following purposes.

1. To break up a long, static scene. Such a scene usu-ally fails to hold the audience unless the director uses some technical means to recapture their attention when it flags. To have an actor change his position is a very effective way of accomplishing this purpose.

2. To change the stage picture. If a group of actors play a long scene in unchanged positions, the audience gets tired of looking at the picture they present. To prevent this the director has one or more of them change positions from time to time during the scene.

3. To recapture attention for an actor. If one of the

characters in a scene has been standing apart from the general action and has taken no part in it, it is necessary to draw the attention of the audience back to him before he again becomes part of the scene. A movement on his part will accomplish this result.

4. To draw attention to a particular place. If something unexpected by the audience is to occur at a particular place on which their attention has not been focused, the movement of an actor to or past that place will draw their attention to the desired area. For example, a character is to appear at a window back stage right and overhear what is being said on the stage. The scene on stage is being played down stage left. If one of the characters crosses over past the window the eyes of the audience will follow him. The cross must be carefully timed so that he passes the window immediately before the other actor appears. This movement is sometimes referred to as "leading the eye."

5. To build a climax. Since, as psychologists tell us, our emotional reactions to stimuli are largely a matter of duplicated muscular responses, even when such responses are merely "blocked muscular patterns," physical action is a large and important element in creating emotional response and the more movement in a scene the greater amount of emotional response in the audience. This is true, however, only where the climax is one of action; where it is one of thought, the climax may be more effectively built by starting the scene with movement and decreasing it gradually to the point of absolute stillness.

6. To relieve strain. In a long scene of great suspense

it is often desirable to afford a certain amount of relaxation in order that the emotional tension of the audience may not be strained to the breaking point. Movement will sometimes afford the necessary relaxation without dropping the scene.

Motivation. The director may use imposed movement for any or all of the above technical reasons but his technical purpose must never be apparent to the audience. There must always be some reason that makes it seem natural for the character to move as he does at that particular moment. Such a reason may be found in the emotional quality of the dialogue. It may be supplied by special business invented to create it, or it may be innate in the character of the person who moves. In addition to being convincingly motivated imposed movement must be carefully planned so that it is characteristic of the scene and people. To use movement that is uncharacteristic is just as unconvincing as to use movement that is unmotivated.

Movement Values

The terms, weak and strong, as applied to movement have the same attention-value connotation as when used with regard to areas, but they also denote an added element of emotion.

Movement is the simplest way of attracting attention—it will take attention away from speech so that even a weak movement has considerable attention-value. Again the terms are relative and a weak movement has somewhat less attention-value than a strong one. If it is necessary to have one actor move while another speaks a weak move is less apt to distract from the speech than a strong one.

The emotional element involved in the terms *is not the amount of emotion but the kind*. A weak movement may express a very great embarrassment or a powerful feeling of fear or horror. On the other hand a strong movement may express mild curiosity, or anticipation. The "strongest" feeling of fear would never be expressed by a strong movement, nor the "weakest" feeling of anger by a weak movement.

Again we want to insist that there is no idea of good or bad, right or wrong, definite or indefinite involved in the use of these terms.

Strong Movements. Strong movements are forward movements, that is toward the audience, or movements such as rising from a sitting position or going up steps, that take an actor from one level to a higher one.

The forward movements, listed with the strongest first, are up center to down center, up right or up left to down center, the full stage diagonals, from up right or up left to the opposite down stage position, down left or down right, and the movements from right or left to center parallel to the curtain line at any level.

Weak Movements. Weak movements are the opposite of strong, that is backward movements away from the audience and descending movements, sitting, stooping, coming down stairs, etc.

The old "actor's paradox" occurs, however, in this matter. Weakness on the stage must not be weak weakness, but strong weakness. That is a weak movement must be positively weak and not weak through indecision or ineffectiveness.

The backward movements, listed with the weakest first, are from down center to up center, from down right or down left to up center, the full stage diagonals that is from down right or left to up left or up right, and from center to left or right on any level.

Neutral Movements. The movements clear across the stage from right to left or from left to right are neutral as far as direction is concerned. That is they are neither markedly strong nor weak except as some other element enters in to give them one value or the other. In spite of this neutrality they seem to have a slightly different value. Most people feel that the movement from right to left is slightly stronger than the movement from left to right, that is that it is easier to make right to left a strong movement and left to right a weak one. The explanation may be that our eyes, trained by our manner of reading, move naturally from left to right, that is from Stage Right to Stage Left.

It sometimes happens that there are two conflicting values in a movement which neutralize each other. For instance, an actor ascends a staircase (a strong movement) that runs along the right wall from down right to up left (a backward and therefore weak direction). The movement will therefore be neutral unless some other element gives it strength, or weakness. It is well for the director to recognize such a possible neutralization in planning the set.

One of the "other elements" that affects most decidedly the value of movements is the presence of a second actor placed in a direct relationship to the actor moving. The full stage cross from right to left or from left to right becames definitely strong when the moving actor approaches another, weak when he moves away from the other. The weak diagonals from down stage to up stage are strengthened when the second actor is approached. The strong forward movements, because the moving actor is in such positive relation to the audience, are not perceptibly weakened even though another actor be left unless the moving actor backs away. The backing away of one actor from another is always a weak movement. It is often a very definite and effective movement expressing a great degree of emotion, but it will only be effective if the emotion to be expressed is weak in quality. Parallel and counter movements of two actors are apt to appear awkward and such awkwardness will immediately destroy their original values. They frequently appear funny and this comedy value can be effectively used in the broader types of comedy and farce. The same is true when one actor immediately follows another, but if the first actor is followed by a group, moving as a unit, it is not true. The difference in size of the two moving elements, the actor and the group, serves to break their close and immediate association in our minds, and to give them a more even balance.

In considering the relative value of movements we have so far neglected the most important factor. *The manner in which an actor moves affects the resulting strength or weakness of the movement far more than its direction.* If, however, the manner of moving and the value inherent in the direction of the movement can be made to coincide the effect of the manner of moving will be emphasized. If they do not coincide, the effect of the manner, even though it predominates, may be decidedly lessened by the counter-acting value of the movement.

MOVEMENTS FOR COMPENSATION

The terms "to dress stage," "to counter" and "to give" are applied to movements of compensation. When one actor moves it is often necessary to have another move slightly in order to keep from being covered, to clear for the movement of the first actor or to maintain a balanced stage picture. To dress stage and to counter mean practically the same thing. Some directors prefer one term, some the other. Such movements are used for the latter purpose of maintaining a balanced picture. To give is usually a slight movement, perhaps just a step, back and away to allow for the approach or passing of another actor. These movements should be unobtrusive and while making them the actor should usually maintain a steady focus on the center of interest. They are frequently motivated by a desire to see or hear better what is occurring among the other characters.

TURNS

Many actors find it difficult to turn effectively and without awkwardness. It is simply a matter of the positions of the feet and the shifting of weight and the technique can be easily mastered with a little practice.

If the actor is crossing the stage and wishes to turn

back he may do so by using the waltz step except that he lifts his feet instead of gliding. If the turn must be very abrupt, however, he should come to a stop with his weight on his forward foot. If he wishes to turn to his left his right foot should be forward, if to his right, his left foot should be in advance. As soon as he stops he pivots his back foot ninety degrees, shifts his weight onto it and takes the first step in the new direction with the other foot.

To turn from a standing position the weight should be on the foot opposite to the direction in which the actor desires to turn, the other foot should be moved back in a ninety degree arc, the weight shifted to it and the first step made with the other foot.

The Stage Turn. It has been customary for an actor to turn so that his face is toward the audience as he turns. Many directors feel that this piece of technique is outmoded and certainly it is apt to appear artificial if used in the down stage areas, since the actor is turning away from, rather than toward, the other characters on the stage. It usually seems natural enough, however, from up stage areas and it has the advantage of keeping the actor in more direct relation to the audience if he is important in the scene.

QUALITIES OF MOVEMENT

As a general practice movements on the stage should be direct, completed and definite. That is movements should have these qualities unless a desired dramatic effect is gained by their being indirect, uncompleted or wavering. And even then we come back to the actor's paradox. An indirect movement must be made directly.

Direct Movements. An inexperienced actor, perhaps from some almost unconscious feeling of good manners, will usually go around behind people and furniture. Unless it is in character, as perhaps for a servant, such a move is not desirable. A direct cross in front will eliminate the appearance of unnecessary effort, of working too hard, which is fatal in any artistic expression. A straight line is the shortest distance between two points on the stage as well as in geometry. A director, however, may deliberately use the other to achieve an effect.

The Curved Cross. The curved or arc cross is an indirect movement used frequently on the stage for a technical purpose. By its use an actor may move from a down stage position to an actor up stage of him and secure a position above him and facing the audience. Such a move is illustrated in Diagram II A. Another use of the curved cross is to enable an actor to cross from an up stage position to someone down stage of him and give the stage to the other actor. (Diagram II B)

Like the Stage Turn the Curved Cross is sometimes considered old fashioned technique. It has quite definite uses but the director must see that it is never exaggerated and the angle of the arc should be kept as small as possible. In order to use either form of the curved cross the two actors must not be too close together. If the cross is long enough it will not be apparent to the audience that the actor is not moving in a direct line.

Completed Movements. Any movement to be effective on the stage must be large enough to register as a

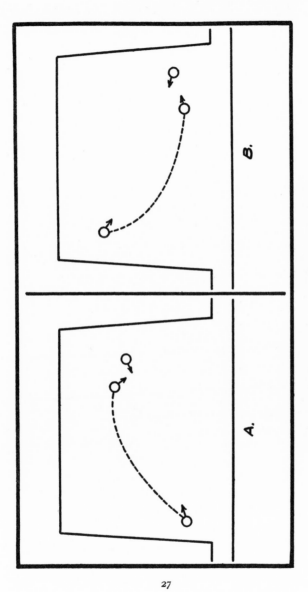

DIAGRAM II - THE CURVE CROSS.

movement. Movements that are started and left incomplete create a fuzzy and meaningless impression.

If a movement is incompleted it must be broken definitely and intentionally. Movements may be stopped by a change of thought on the part of the character, by another character's speech, by something suddenly heard or seen either on stage or off, or in order to speak. Such incompletion is said to be motivated and it explains itself.

Definite Movements. Uncertain or accidental movements are most distracting, and may be the means of ruining an otherwise good scene. Whatever an actor does, whatever moves he makes the audience must feel that he meant to do it. Even a step, unmotivated and uncalled for, or a slight shifting of the body position may distract the audience's attention from the dialogue and set them to wondering what the actor is about to do.

MOVEMENT IN RELATION TO DIALOGUE

One of the most important things for the director to remember in planning both movement and business is that *physical movement takes and holds the attention far more readily than speech*. In planning movement that is to accompany dialogue the director must see that the feeling of the movement and that of the line correspond. There are many lines in every play that are neutral emotionally and on such lines the movement may be either strong or weak, but if the emotion or idea of the line suggests strength then the accompanying movement must be strong, if weakness, then the movement must be weak. (Again it is the quality of the emotion expressed by the line and not its amount that determines its strength or weakness.) Movements that conflict in value with the idea of the line become funny. Such usage is effective only in comedy.

Movement by the Speaker. Since movement attracts attention an actor may move on almost any line that he has to say, unless the emotional quality of the line or its idea suggest stillness, provided his movement is not one of such unusual interest as to detract from his speech. Nevertheless the old theatre adage, not to move on a plot line is a pretty safe one to follow. Since it is absolutely necessary for the audience, in order to follow the story, to hear and comprehend fully the plot lines, it is well to take no chance that their attention may be involved in what the actor is doing rather than in what he is saying.

When an actor moves and speaks at the same time, it is not necessary and frequently not desirable, to have him look at the person to whom he is speaking. It is more natural and usually far less awkward to have him look where he is going. This is especially true when the actor is not approaching directly the person to whom he is speaking.

An actor may move just before he speaks for any of the following reasons.

1. To recapture the attention of the audience if he has been out of the center of interest of the scene.

2. If the movement is strong, in order to emphasize his speech.

3. To build up an exit. This is an old stage practice,

and if such a move is unmotivated it is very artificial. It is frequently desirable for an actor to give his last line before leaving the stage near the exit, but it is much less an obvious trick if the director can have him in that position some little time before he speaks. If, however, there is sufficient motivation for the move just before the line, such a move does serve to emphasize the exit.

4. To indicate the idea that is completed by the line. For example, an actor crosses to a table, the move being followed by the line, "It must be here somewhere."

The speaker may move after his speech in order to change or break the mood or thought, or when the movement completes an idea indicated in the line. "If you'd really rather be alone—" and he crosses to the door.

It is sometimes inevitable that a weak movement must be made at approximately the same time that a strong speech is given. Such a movement will have less effect on the value of the line if it is made after the line is said rather than with the line or even before it.

Movement by an Actor Other than the Speaker. It is frequently necessary to have an actor move while someone else is speaking. Such movements should be unobtrusive and if possible weak in value and the actor moving should usually maintain a focus on the person speaking. They should be carefully timed in order to occur between parts of the speech or on unimportant words or phrases. They should never be made on a plot line. They will not be distracting if the speaker himself is moving. Movements for compensation are of this order. Movements of other actors if they reflect the emotion or thought of the speaker's line may even be used to emphasize those lines.

As a general rule it is unwise to have either actor move during a scene of question and answer unless it is unusually long or unless the emotional quality of the lines definitely suggest movement.

Movement in a Pacing Scene. A scene in which one character strides up and down across the stage during an agitated conversation with another person must be carefully planned both as to timing and direction of the movement. The latter must have variety and must increase in speed and distance covered as the scene reaches its climax. The movement must fit in with the value of the lines, weak move on weak line and strong on strong. This is especially true of the pacer's own lines. Important lines must not be muffled by movement. A weak movement will distract less than a strong one when the other person has the important line. A sudden turn or stop or both will serve to give excellent emphasis to the important lines spoken by the pacer. A change of direction, especially from weak to strong, will have the same effect.

CHAPTER IV

NECESSARY BUSINESS

Every production should present the story of the play graphically as well as audibly. What the audience see is quite as important to their understanding of the play as what they hear. This graphic presentation consists largely of the detailed pantomimic action of the individual characters, and, since visual impressions are apt to be quicker and deeper than auditory, such business cannot be too carefully planned and rehearsed. Unlike movement, the greatest amount of which is usually imposed for purposes other than story telling, the major part of the business of any production is made necessary by the plot. Business is, of course, frequently used to create atmosphere and character or for purely technical purposes, but a too extensive use of business that has nothing to do with the story is apt to be confusing. The director who can plan his necessary business so that it also creates atmosphere and character and accomplishes his technical purposes is working with artistic economy.

Any unusual piece of business on which the plot turns, such as the finding of the missing will, the stealing of money, the drinking of poison, etc., must be unusually carefully planned and timed. If possible it should be pointed or fore-shadowed. It is like a plot line and the audience must not only perceive it but comprehend it.

There are two pieces of necessary business that will be found in every play no matter what its story. They are entrances and exits. The action of the play will always be found to rest to a large extent on who comes and who goes.

ENTRANCES

When an actor enters he must achieve the effect of coming into the actual place presented, not of walking onto the stage. He must come from a definite place, not from the wings. He must enter in character and with the character's situation definitely in mind. Place, situation and character will all influence his manner of entering. Whenever possible have the actor start his entrance four or five feet outside the door that he may have a natural momentum. This will necessitate a cue for starting his walk that comes a second or so earlier than the actual cue for entering the stage. The cue for actual entrance will, unless he comes on speaking, come a second or so at least before the first speech cue.

The actor should assume relationship with the characters already on the stage the instant he enters. Even when he is supposed to be unaware of their presence that very unawareness constitutes a relationship.

Above all the actor on entering must create "the illusion of the first time." No one knows when he opens the door of a room, even though he has only been gone for a few moments, just what he will find on entering. The people that he left there may have died of heart-failure or at least they may have changed their seats. The well-rehearsed actor is apt to forget this fact. He has entered the room so many times during rehearsal that he forgets that he has no reason to expect John to whom he speaks first to be standing by the fireplace. The means of creating this illusion is an acute awareness on the actor's part that he has never been in that room before under just those circumstances. The inexperienced actor may strive to give the desired impression by a pause and a look about, but this is apt to appear decidedly artificial.

Entrances with Lines. The playwright does not bring an actor onto the stage until he is ready to use him as a vital part of his scene, either for what he does or for what he hears or for what he says. If then, an actor has a line to say immediately after his entrance, it is natural to have him say it near the door. If he waits to reach some definite position farther on stage, the action of the play stops while he makes the cross. Of course there are instances when something in the situation or business requires him to speak from somewhere else than near the door. That is a problem in timing for the director.

Entrances without Lines. Since the actor only comes on the stage when he is needed by the playwright as part of the scene it is necessary for the audience to be aware of his presence immediately. If the other characters are aware of his entrance the matter is comparatively simple. A quick entrance and sudden stop, the sound of the closing door, or any noise will accomplish the purpose. If, however, the other characters are to remain unaware of his presence, the matter of attracting the attention of the audience to him becomes more difficult. Any noise would of course attract the attention of the other characters as well as that of the audience. A quick movement and sudden stop would also attract their attention, or the audience feels as though it would. The entrance of course must be, or appear to be, out of the line of vision of the other actors. Placing it in a strong area, such as up stage center, will help. Sometimes the actor may put his head in first, withdraw, and then enter. The added amount of movement, movement designed to express caution, is a means of attracting attention. Better, perhaps, if possible, is to have him appear first at a window and then enter. The movement for "leading the eye," made by one of the characters already on stage, may be used to point his appearance at the window. If the window is large enough, a quick, positive move across it will usually be sufficient to draw the attention of the audience. The plot situation which makes such an entrance necessary will often suggest the correct way to handle it. The director must take such an entrance into consideration in planning the layout for his set.

Built Entrances. The highly emphasized or "built" entrance was, and often still is, used when the production was made about one or two great actors, and designed as a vehicle for them. In modern ensemble playing and especially in a realistic play, the use of such a built entrance seems extremely artificial and undesirable, unless the emphasizing is very carefully and unobtrusively done. In a less realistic type of play, such as certain stylized productions, farce, melodrama, costume plays or the classics, or in a production in which the director is emphasizing the theatric values, such built up entrances are not only desirable but necessary.

An entrance may be built by the use of any of the following means or by a combination of two or more of them.

1. The characters may be so grouped on the stage that they form a line or lines that lead the eyes of the audience toward the door. If it can be arranged so that the characters are facing or turn to face the door just before the entrance the emphasis is still greater.

2. A playwright's device for building an entrance is to have the character speak off stage and someone on stage mention his name. Such an instance sometimes occurs in a play where a built entrance is not desired by the director, in which case the lines must be softened, either in the reading or by some technical means such as counter-focus.

3. An announcement, either formal or informal, indicated of course in the script, may be followed by a perceptible pause. This is a good method of building suspense provided the pause is carefully and adequately motivated. If it is not accounted for the audience is likely to wonder what has gone wrong.

4. A pause following a knock at the door may be used if it can be motivated. Having one of the characters on stage cross to open the door will serve as motivation for the pause. The knock alone without the pause will emphasize an entrance somewhat.

5. A character entering in a brilliant costume, or one

in strong contrast to the others present, will attract the attention of the audience immediately.

6. A bright light, seen off stage as soon as the door opens, will focus the eyes of the audience on the doorway. If the door can be opened before the actual entrance the pointing will be even more effective.

7. A character may be seen off stage through a window or door before his entrance.

8. An unbalanced stage picture, with the actors grouped on the side of the stage opposite the door, if it is held long enough before the entrance of an important character tends to create an unconscious feeling on the part of the audience that something is going to happen, or ought to happen, that will supply the missing element and balance the group. If a minor character, a servant perhaps, comes in and during a short scene balances the picture, the fact that the thing needed for such a balance is the entrance of another person will also be subconsciously suggested to the audience. The lack of balance in the picture must be very decided and a definite reason for the grouping used must be indicated.

9. An entrance made at the top of a flight of stairs or on any higher level will be pointed by the increased strength of the area in which it is made. Remember, however, that the movement of descending the steps may be weak and hold it until the actor can descend without counteracting the effect of his strong, pointed entrance.

10. The sudden stopping of all dialogue, especially if it has been very animated, will draw attention to a character making an entrance. This may be used effectively with the change of focus mentioned under #1.

11. If two people are to enter the least important character may come in first, turn and look at the door.

12. If a group enters the person whose entrance it is desirable to emphasize should be placed last. The character of next greatest importance will receive better attention if he comes first.

13. Belasco used to build the entrance of his star by having the electrician bring up the intensity of general illumination on the stage immediately on the star's entrance. If this method is used, it must be very carefully handled. The increase must come slowly and the intensity should not be brought up over a point or so by dimmer reading. In other words the audience should feel and react to the added brightness without being consciously aware of it.

Exits

The actor must use the same care to remain in character when he leaves the stage that he uses when he enters it. Too often an inexperienced actor goes out in a manner that suggests he may be saying to himself, "Thank goodness, that scene's over!" He drops his character with his last speech. Instead he should imagine vividly the place to which he is going and his reason for going there.

The giving of the actor's last or exit line near the door will enable him to leave the stage without loss of time so that the scene immediately following may take place without any hold. In many, many instances, however, the manner with which the actor crosses to the door and goes out may be a dramatic means of emphasizing either the situation or the character. When the manner of making exit is thus effective there is no feeling of held action even though the dialogue of the next scene is delayed by a second or so.

When the actor crosses from center or the opposite side of the stage, the movement should be in a direct line unless there is strong motivation for its being indirect. If, however, the actor is moving from a down stage position to a door on the opposite side of the stage but up stage of his original position the use of the curved cross will keep him opened up.

When two people make an exit together, the actor who has the lines usually goes first. This gives him a motive for turning back slightly to the person behind him so that his line will be delivered more toward the audience and not into the wall of the set.

Handling Doors

Many actors, awkward at nothing else, are awkward when it comes to opening a stage door. The following simple rule will prevent such awkwardness, if the door is hinged up stage and opens off as most stage doors are and do.

Open the door with the up stage hand, enter, make a quarter turn toward the audience, and close it with the down stage hand.

To enter a door in the back wall, open it with the hand on the side of the hinges and close it with the right hand if it is desirable to have the body turned to the right, with the left hand if it is desirable to have the body turned toward the left.

Doors hinged to open on stage may be handled in the same manner, except, of course, that the actor must come farther on stage and will probably have to make a slight step back in order to close the door.

If the actor is carrying something large, such as a suitcase, he can carry it in his up stage hand and use the down stage hand both to open and close the door. If he must enter carrying something that takes both hands, as a large tray, it is better either to have the door left open for him or to have some other character in the scene open it for him. Do not let someone in the wings do it. Plan the business so that he is able to set down his burden and then close the door.

In making an exit a door at the side should be opened with the up stage hand, a door in the back wall with either the right or left hand according to which direction it is desirable to have the actor's body turned just before he goes out.

Curtains. If an actor has to make an entrance through curtains or portieres that lap at the opening, he should enter parallel to the curtains, holding the back lap away from the front and letting it drop as he passes between. This will keep the curtains from pulling apart. If there is no need to keep the curtains closed, one part may simply be pulled back so that it may drop into place again after the entrance or exit. If the curtains are hung from rings that slide easily on the pole, the one to be opened should be grasped low down and lifted before being pulled back. This removes the weight from the rings and prevents their sliding out of place, causing the curtain to remain open after it is dropped.

To make an exit through curtains when the opening is not visible, the actor should not grope about to find it. A slight but sharp rap on the curtains will cause them to divide, thus disclosing the opening. The actor should then exit parallel to them in the same manner described for entering.

PLACING OF EXITS AND ENTRANCES

In planning the stage set careful attention should be given to the dramatic value of exits and entrances and the position of doors decided with this in mind. Of course the rules of architecture must not be violated either. Nothing is more distracting than a set whose doors and windows are placed in positions that would obviously be impossible in any actual building. Important and strong entrances are most effective if made through a door at the back. Important exits, on the other hand, are more easily handled through a door down stage left or right. If a weak exit is desired again a door at the back is desirable. If the same door must be used on two occasions that conflict in feeling, as, for example, a strong entrance and a strong exit, the director must decide which occasion is most important and place the door accordingly. Other factors, aside from its position, such as levels and light, may be used to determine the value of an entrance. If a door in the back wall opens on to steps that lead directly down stage, an entrance made through it will be strengthened because of the higher level. The two elements that are involved in the actor's movement after the entrance, that is the forward direction (strong) and the higher to

lower level (weak), neutralize each other and leave it
definitely up to the actor to give the movement its value
by his manner of moving. The same is true of the movement by which the actor approaches the door. Such an
arrangement, therefore, may be used as a solution for a
problem of conflicting exits and entrances.

Because of the importance of elements such as these
it is well for the scene designer to accept the floor plan
from the director before preparing his sketches. The
director should not let even the most beautiful set design
interfere in any way with the elements necessary to the
action of the play. On the other hand a good scene designer's suggestions often prove most valuable and helpful and his knowledge may prevent the director from
doing the architecturally impossible. A close cooperation between the two artists is most desirable.

THE USE OF FURNITURE

Next to entrances and exits, the most common form
of business has to do with the use of furniture. Except
for some of the classic dramas, nearly all plays require
furniture of some sort. Even an outdoor set has its
fallen logs, its big stones and its tree roots that serve as
seats. An important element in securing an easy and
natural production is to make sure that your actors treat
the furniture in a natural manner. Do not be afraid to
have them move it about, but be sure that they know
accurately just where it is to be placed. On a small stage,
especially, a question of inches may matter. It often
helps the naturalness of a scene to have some of the

furniture out of place—that is where it will not be used in the course of the scene—at the opening and have the characters arrange it as the action progresses. Such business is usually limited to chairs and small tables; it must always be confined to pieces that can be easily handled by the characters.

The director should watch for and check any slight, ineffective and unnecessary movement of furniture by the actors. It is often done from nervousness and is very apt to create a feeling of restlessness and to prove distracting.

In moving about the stage actors should learn to relate themselves to the furniture. Anyone approaching close to a table or chair, for instance, is apt to touch it, lean on it or relate himself to it in some way. Such business may appear to be entirely unconscious on the part of the character, but if he omits it the effect is often stiff and unreal. The opposite mistake, of course, is to have the actor always stay in such close relationship to the various pieces of furniture as to give the idea that he needs them for support. Very inexperienced players are perhaps more apt to err in this way than the other because of stage fright or nervousness.

Seating the Actors. If you are handling a group it is never very pleasing or convincing to have them all take seats at the same time unless such a piece of business is definitely indicated in the dialogue.

If an actor is standing immediately in front of the chair in which he is to sit, he should not turn to look at it before he sits down. In most cases the scene requires that his eyes be elsewhere, and even if it does not such a glance is apt to over point the business of sitting. If the actor is not sure of the chair's position he can move back very slightly until he feels it with the calf of his leg. When possible it is better to let the actor approach the chair in which he is to sit directly, even if the move only necessitates one or two short steps.

Sitting Positions. A good sitting position for a woman is with one foot slightly in front of the other. This may be varied by crossing the ankles. The angle of the sight lines from the audience usually makes it inadvisable to sit with crossed legs, unless the character is such as calls for some such expression of vulgarity.

A man's natural action of pulling up his trousers before he sits down is apt to seem too important on the stage, and, again, the sight lines bring too much ankle into view when trousers are so treated. If the man sits with his feet in the same plane the position will always be acceptable. Crossed legs, especially if the foot off the floor is pointed down stage, are apt to present a large amount of shoe sole to the audience's view.

When an actor has to sit in a chair placed with its back three quarters to the audience, he may play more directly to the audience by arranging his body in the chair at a different angle. (Diagram III A) This necessitates sitting forward in the chair. In playing from such a position to another actor farther up stage the head may be turned toward him and the body also occasionally but the down stage actor need not really face nor turn to the person he addresses. The slight turn mentioned will create the illusion desired.

When two actors are seated on a sofa placed at an

DIAGRAM III — SITTING POSITION.

45

angle to the audience the one to the up stage end should sit forward, the down stage actor, well back. (Diagram III B)

Rising. To get up easily from a sitting position the actor should have the up stage foot forward and use the down stage foot for the push, letting the weight shift to the forward foot as he comes up. The first step is then taken with the down stage foot.

Furniture Used for Dramatic Effect. The placing of a table or some other piece of furniture between two people engaged in a dispute or argument will markedly increase the feeling of conflict.

Mechanics for Handling a Table Scene. Playwrights have a great fondness for showing their characters at a meal and such a scene usually presents many difficulties for the director.

In a realistic play people should sit on all four sides of the table, except in the case of a head table at a banquet, royalty, etc. Do not be afraid to seat people with their backs to the audience, keeping, of course, the more important characters up stage. A round table makes it possible to steal a little on the positions in order to open up. If the scene is an important one and the characters have to remain about the table for some time, it is advisable to use a triangular set. (Diagram IV A) If you must use a square or oblong table, it helps to rake the side walls of the set and place the table parallel to one of them. (Diagram IV B)

When two people are at the table it is natural for them to sit opposite each other. If, however, the scene definitely belongs to one of them he can be placed up

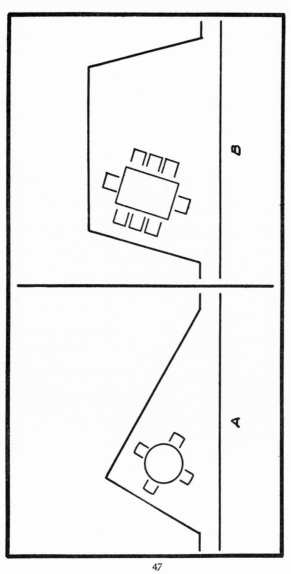

DIAGRAM IV – TABLE SCENES.

47

stage of the table and the other character seated on his right or left. This position is an unusual one for husband and wife.

In directing a scene in which a group of people are seated on all sides of a table there are certain "tricks" that will be found helpful. The use of higher chairs or chairs with cushions in them on the up stage side of the table will help to keep the people seated in them from being covered. The people seated on the down stage side need not look directly at the others when they speak. Because of the sight angles this fact will not be noticeable to the audience, unless it is overdone. Watch for the earliest opportunity to open up the scene and take, or make, an excuse to have the down stage people leave the table as soon as they convincingly can.

The author rarely allows sufficient time for the actual eating of a meal. The director can sometimes cover this fact by the menu he plans. In any case all stage food must be soft and easy to chew and care must be taken that nothing is served that might tend to irritate the throats of the actors. It is well to have several rehearsals with the actual food. If you do not you may find either that your actors are eating nothing at all or that, because they are eating, the desired tempo of the scene has been dropped. The eating of food must be carefully timed; each actor should know just what he can eat and when. The serving of the meal, if it is done by servants, must also be most carefully timed. Neither the eating nor the serving should be allowed to interfere with or muffle the dialogue.

Use of Hand Properties

Even when the author spares the director the problem of serving a regular meal, he is apt to succumb to the temptation of tea or cocktails. Such scenes give a lifelike and realistic atmosphere especially if the details are carefully planned and worked out. The atmosphere created by such business is paid for too dearly, however, if the business distracts in any way from more essential action or from dialogue. Time it carefully so that it does not block the lines but keep it unhurried. Dialogue should not be held for such reasons as drinking, lighting a cigarette, etc. unless the pause, filled by such business, is dramatically desirable.

The use of hand properties in such scenes as those just mentioned is usually made necessary by the script, but the director will frequently find them useful even when they are not actually called for by the author. The picking up of a book or magazine, the readjustment of small ornaments, the patting into shape of pillows, and the handling of personal properties such as powder compact, cigarette, watch, etc., all serve as means by which the director can help enliven a static scene or motivate a changed stage picture. Any business so used must be thoroughly motivated and care must be taken that it is neither stereotyped nor artificial. The technical purpose for which it is used should never be apparent.

Pointing an Important Property

If the story of the play is closely connected with a stage or hand property, it should be carefully pointed early in the play. The expert playwright usually does this, at least to a certain extent, in the dialogue, but the director must reinforce such pointing or supply it when it is missing. The careful placing of the piece of furniture or hand property in a strong area where it will attract attention, or the planning of definite and interesting business in which it is involved will serve as means of planting it in the minds of the audience so that its use at the vital moment is prepared for.

BUSINESS FOR LOVE SCENES

The director using inexperienced players will find love scenes difficult. Actors who sustain their roles well at all other times are apt to drop out of character and become self-conscious the minute they are expected to make love. It is often well to rehearse such scenes separately until the actors gain some assurance. The choice of the playing area and picturization of the emotions involved through the positions of the actors and through appropriate business are important elements in making a love scene effective. The poorer the actors, the more the director will have to depend on his own creation of picture and business to carry the scene. A very romantic play, too, calls for a greater use of these elements than a realistic play.

Love scenes, unless very short, usually are more effective played about a piece of furniture; a large chair, a piano, a bench without a back, etc. are all excellent. The director should be very careful in his use of a sofa. In the first place it is used very frequently and it is somewhat difficult to create business around it that does not seem stereotyped. It can, however, be used effectively for a kneeling embrace or for a scene played across the back. It is usually awkward to have both lovers seated on a sofa, especially if there is to be an embrace. A stairway or fireplace will afford opportunities for interesting picturization and business.

The director will often help his scene by choosing a weak area that has picture value and romanticising it as much as possible. The use of firelight, candle-light or moonlight through a window, or the choice of a piece of furniture such as a piano that has romantic associations will help create the illusion desired. Such associations may be innate in the piece of furniture, as in the case of the piano, or they may have been established through careful pointing earlier in the play.

In planning a love scene it is usually advisable to start your lovers at a distance from each other and have them approach each other gradually as the scene progresses. Be careful how and when you seat them; to have them both sit down at once is apt to appear awkward. Avoid opening a love scene with an embrace, unless the script necessitates it, since it leaves little with which to build. In fact the withholding of the embrace until late in the scene is an excellent means of creating suspense. Of course the director will find many love scenes in which it may not be practical to follow these suggestions, but the general principles of romanticised picturization and business can always be applied.

Embraces. The dance position is always a safe and pleasing one to use for a standing embrace. It should however be varied according to the relative position of the lovers. That is the man's up stage arm should be around the woman, the woman's up stage hand on the man's shoulder. The feet of the actors should be close together, otherwise the bodies assume a triangular form that is very displeasing. The approach for a standing embrace should be rehearsed with careful attention to the foot positions. If the actors are very inexperienced it softens such an embrace to have it occur back of a piece of furniture.

A kneeling embrace from the floor is often effective, but it too needs careful rehearsing for positions, especially if the woman is standing. The man's kneeling position must be close to her; it is extremely awkward if he has to reach for her. The kneeling embrace is easier and the actors do not have to be quite so close if the woman is seated. It is perhaps easier and most effective of all when made before a sofa or bench or across the arm of a large chair.

Even more important than the way an embrace is made is the way it is broken. Unless motivated by an interruption the break must be gradual and unhurried. The method used over and over again on both stage and screen is to have the man slowly loosen his clasp, bring his hands to the woman's shoulders or upper arms and then slide his hands down the arms until he is holding her hands in his. Another effective way to break an embrace gradually is for one of the lovers to turn slightly and for them both to move away from the position of the embrace with the man's arm still about the woman.

Kisses. It is frequently wise to mask kisses, especially if the actors are inexperienced. This is easily done by careful attention to the position of the heads or by having the man take the woman's face in his hands. When carefully masked, there need be no actual kiss. This frequently relieves embarrassment for players of little experience and it also prevents trouble from heavily applied lipstick. If the kiss is not masked, and there are many instances when it should not be, it must be rehearsed carefully so that the lips meet directly.

In a love scene where a series of kisses or embraces are used, the principles of climax and variety must be kept in mind. Each kiss or embrace should be different from the others and each succeeding embrace or kiss should be held longer than the one preceding. These suggestions are also, of course, subject to the requirements of the individual scene.

The one essential thing for the director to remember is not to let the actors rush a love scene. It is a tendency which, owing to self-consciousness, they frequently show and the director must anticipate and check it at once.

Business for Stage Fights

Because of the danger involved, the business for a stage fight must be carefully worked out, timed *and set*. Never permit any unplanned fighting. You can get a more spontaneous effect from carefully routined business because the actor does not need to think of what he is going to do nor have done to him and is free to devote himself to creating the spirit of the scene.

A stage fight must be planned to create suspense. The start may be prolonged by detailed business, the characters taking plenty of time to prepare, stripping off coats, etc., but the dialogue must either be continuous through this part of the scene, or at least so carefully interspersed with it that the tension does not drop. After "the battle is joined" the following steps will work successfully for almost any physical struggle:

1. Definite struggle resulting in a draw.
2. Break and pause.
3. Second attack in which the winner of the fight gets the better.
4. Break and shorter pause.
5. Third attack in which the loser gets the better decidedly.
6. Break. If a pause is used it should be very short.
7. Final struggle which may be quickly over or prolonged but which must be obviously decisive.

A struggle, long enough to be convincing as a fight, and put on without breaks will overstrain and snap the audience tension. The breaks give the audience a chance to wonder what is coming next and are invaluable in the creation of suspense. They may be used for giving necessary lines.

In a stage fight the person attacking must be free to do so strenuously. The responsibility for meeting or avoiding the attack lies with the other person. In the same way, in a struggle to escape, the responsibility for preventing it must rest with the captors and the captive must be allowed to make every possible effort to free himself from them. It occasionally happens that you have a stage fight in which the hero is defeated. Care must be taken not to use business that will make him appear abject. He must remain heroic even in defeat. In a scene of bullying, one knock-down blow is usually sufficient. The rest may be done with feints and threats. The audience soon becomes disgusted, if blow after blow is struck and there is no come-back.

When a fight involves physical blows care must be taken in placing them. It is very easy for serious injury to result from a blow, especially the blow of a fist, if it is not carefully directed toward the less vulnerable parts of the body. It is best to use the hollow hand for slapping, both because of the sound it makes and the fact that it is less apt to hurt. It is often possible to place one of the spectators of the fight close enough to the combatants and in such a position that he can supply the sound of the bow by clapping his hands. In this way the actual blow need not be as severe as it appears.

If the fight is prolonged or strenuous or of great importance in the play the director should get an expert to routine it for him along general lines supplied by the director. The results will be surer and less open to technical criticism. This is especially true of sword play, but in such a fight your actors, too, must know how to fence. Sword play can never be convincingly faked.

In staging a fight, set in an interior, try to select stage properties that will stand hard treatment and knocking about. It adds to the reality and excitement if a chair goes over or a table is upset.

Business for Death Scenes

It is generally wiser either to play a death scene in a weak area or with the actor in a weak position, that is, turned from the audience, or both. A strong area may be used when the death scene is the climax of the play and followed almost at once by the curtain. It may also perhaps be used for a very famous death scene in an old play, such as that of "Camille," provided the director has implicit faith in the ability of his actor or actress. Ordinarily, however, the weak area and position should both be used if the scene is to continue after the character's death. The less attention a living corpse receives the better. In any event the physical manifestations of death are not only difficult for the actor to simulate convincingly, but also they are apt to be offensive to the audience and it is therefore advisable to use every means of softening them. Certain death scenes are especially harrowing, as for instance the death of a little child or a violent murder, and the greatest care must be taken by the director that their effect on the audience is not so horrible that it breaks their illusion.

An inexperienced actor will need much directing in order to play a death scene convincingly. Instead of relaxing his body entirely he will probably want to become stiff and rigid. It is advisable to invite a doctor or some other trustworthy authority to supervise the playing of a death scene, since deaths from different causes have different manifestations. Just how many of these manifestations he will use or how accurately strive to portray them, the director will decide on the basis of good taste and judgment. Certainly it is better to sacrifice a realism that only the medical profession has knowledge of, than to break the illusion of reality in the minds of the audience by using too gruesome or harrowing details. If the play is a modern one and a doctor is involved in the scene, the director may well seek expert advice as to the intricacies of a doctor's business on such an occasion. Picturization and carefully planned and rehearsed business will help greatly in making a death scene convincing and they may be depended upon to help carry the scene when the actor is unable to do so fully.

If the body must be removed, you must have sufficient people to do it without its becoming awkward and funny. Four people are better than two. The tenseness of the audience following a death scene may find relief in laughter with very little provocation. If the removal is not necessitated by the play, it is much better to have the death occur in a weak area and the actor placed so that he is at least partly hidden from the audience by a high chair back, a screen, etc. and then to move the other characters away into a strong area for the rest of the scene. The audience's attention will follow the moving, speaking characters and they will have very little notice to spare for the dead person.

Scenes of Violent Death. Much of the technique suggested for use in stage fights will be found helpful in directing a scene of violent death.

When death results from stabbing, it is better to mask the act of stabbing than to use a fake knife. Be sure to dull the edge of the real knife. Put the person to be killed down stage and have the killer approach him from above.

If the killer makes a sudden move immediately preced ing the stabbing the eyes of the audience will be distracted from the knife and they are not so apt to see the actual blow. The knife is frequently passed between the arm and the body of the victim. It is easier to mask the act of stabbing if the victim is facing the audience and has his back to the killer but this is, naturally, not always possible. If the stabbing is masked by quick sure movements you can miss the victim's body without much danger of being detected.

The manner in which the knife is removed has as much to do with creating the illusion of stabbing as anything else. It should be pulled out as though it came hard, and thrown away, covered or wiped quickly, before the audience has a chance to notice the absence of blood.

The victim of a stabbing should not collapse at once. There should be a static moment. His immediate reaction is to reach for the wound. If he can stagger to a piece of furniture and let himself down to one knee before he actually collapses it is less of a jar to the audience than if he pitches forward from a standing position. (This, by the way, is excellent technique to use for a fainting scene.) When the victim falls he should keep his feet fast to the floor and fall so that the soles of his feet are not toward the audience. If he can fall with his head to center stage it is better. His body can relax into a comfortable position after the fall. It often helps if he can be killed near a door, catch the frame and fall off stage, thus eliminating the problem of removal. If he must remain on stage it is well to have him collapse back of a table, desk, davenport, or rather large piece of furniture, thus being hidden or partly hidden from the audience after death.

Many of the foregoing suggestions are applicable to a shooting scene. In such a scene the killer and his victim should be as far apart as possible. There is danger of injury even from a gun loaded with a blank if it is fired at too close range. The gun should be pointed at the ground, never directly at the other actor. The stage manager should be provided with a cover gun of the same bore as that used by the actor. He should stand where he can see the action on the stage, if that is at all possible, and if the actor's gun should miss fire, he can cover the contretemps by firing his own gun. Such cover fire is not usually apparent to the audience. At least it is not near as obvious as no sound at all when a man is supposed to be shot. When guns, either loaded or unloaded, are carried about the stage, care should be taken that they never point toward the audience. To have a gun pointed at you even unintentionally from the stage is apt to break illusion by creating a feeling of alarm.

INCIDENTAL SPECIALTIES

Music, songs, dances, etc. interpolated in the action of a play must be very carefully handled by the director to keep them in focus and make them an integral part of the scene. Such business should be played to the people on the stage and never to the audience unless the play is frankly theatrical or belongs to and is directed in the manner of a past period when that style of playing prevailed. In a modern, realistic play such a specialty blends in better if it can begin a little before the dialogue quite stops. It should begin gently, slowly and in a subdued tone and it is kept in focus better if given in a weak area. At least it may begin and end in one. After the number is over the dialogue should begin at once or perhaps even a little before the end. In the case of a song or a dance the accompaniment, both at beginning and end, can often be used as a means of blending. The proper timing and blending of such an interpolation will serve to kill any applause from the audience which, though it may be gratifying to the performer, is undesirable since it usually gives too great significance to the scene. The performer should never acknowledge such applause for an acknowledgment will still further break the illusion.

Incidental specialties should be short and, if possible, unfamiliar. A too familiar number has personal associations for the audience which destroy illusion. A very popular number is almost sure to bring applause. Also one that is too spectacular. If the dramatist has indicated special music or a particular song which the director feels is too familiar or spectacular he can sometimes select another which has the emotional quality desired without the drawback.

Soloists should be in position and instruments should be tuned before the cue for starting the number. At the close of the number the performer should hold his position until the dialogue is well started. In the case of a song or dance the source of the accompaniment should be logically accounted for.

Pantomimic Conversations

It is never convincing to see people talking in pantomime in an area from which we have just heard or are
about to hear audible speech, yet in handling a large
group such pantomime is often inevitable. As a general
rule it is better to try to have all the people on the stage
focused on and interested in the speakers, but, of course,
there are scenes in which this is neither possible nor desirable. In many instances the director can invent business other than pantomimed conversation that will take
care of the characters who must be out of the scene.
When, however, pantomimed conversations seem right
or inevitable it is well to try to reserve certain up stage
areas for them. If such a pantomimic conversation blends
into audible speech from the same characters, move them
down stage as their lines begin to be heard. If you cannot reserve certain areas entirely for the pantomimic conversations try at least not to have audible speech given
from them either immediately before or immediately
after the pantomimic scene. In handling a mob scene it
is often possible to design the set so that there is or seems
to be a division between the areas used for the audible
principals and the inaudible, but apparently conversing
throng. If the mob can be seen through doors and windows, beyond an arcade or even back of a rail fence the
audience will have the subconscious feeling that there is
a reason why they can be seen to talk but can not be
heard.

Of course, there are productions where the dialogue
jumps from group to group and where only short

speeches or fragments of speeches are heard from each. This is a form of expressionism in the writing and the director cannot achieve entire naturalism in the direction of such a scene. He can approach it if the situation permits his keeping a low hum or buzz of conversation from the entire company all the time with the speech fragments coming out over it. If this is not possible, or if it interferes with the clarity of the story, the director must depend on the life and vitality of his pantomime to create the illusion of reality in the audience.

CHAPTER V

IMPOSED BUSINESS

In addition to the graphic presentation of the story, business is used by both the director and the actor for other purposes. It is one of the most effective means of creating character and both director and actor should be constantly observant of manners, mannerisms and "the various ways that various things are done" in order to enrich their work on the stage. The director uses business as an important element in creating the atmosphere or locale in which his play is set, and he sometimes inserts it for a purely technical reason. It is desirable when possible, to achieve these purposes by the use of business that also forwards the story and business used for other reasons must never interfere in kind or amount with that necessary to the plot.

Business Used to Create Atmosphere

In designing business to suggest the locale of the play the director must be careful to choose such acts as are most typical of the region presented. Even common, ordinary, everyday acts are done differently in different countries and in different parts of the same country. The more a director knows about customs and social usage the richer his production will be. In producing a play set in a locale unknown or only slightly known to the director, considerable research should precede any actual work on the production. The racial and national characteristics of the people presented, must of course be taken into consideration, in the invention of business for them, and this is true when such characters appear, either in a group or singly, in an environment that is not native to them.

Special conditions supposed to exist at the time of the action will also influence the business. The actions of the same man when he is very cold or suffering from heat will be entirely different, a fact that many actors neglect in planning their business. Darkness or gloom, moisture, snow, the presence of filth and vermin and many other special conditions will influence the kind of business used.

Another important element is time. Even a short period of years will often change manners and customs. In producing a play of a past period the director must watch his actors carefully to see that the customary and habitual manners of the present do not creep in. The substitution of business typical of the period presented in the early rehearsals is the easiest, surest and most effective way to eliminate such anachronisms. Again research should precede production if the director is not thoroughly familiar with the period.

Extras. In order to create a natural atmosphere in scenes where people are apt to come and go, scenes such as a street, a village green, a church, a railway station, etc. the director often introduces characters that have nothing to do with the story of the play. It is usually good to keep such people in weak areas. Their coming and going must be carefully timed not to distract from or blur the action of the play and their business should be kept in the background and subdued. These suggestions apply only to use of extras for atmospheric purposes and are not valid when they are a vital part of the play.

Business to Suggest Character

Business that delineates character should come in a large degree from the actor, since he is the interpretive artist of his own role. The director should encourage his actors to create their own business, but he must be ready to suggest and advise when the actor's imagination fails. Business created by the actor is likely to have more spontaneity than that supplied by the director but the director must check it constantly to see that it is in keeping with his interpretation of the play and does not blur other values. Correct timing is an important element in an actor's use of personal business. A sharper character usually results when the actor uses a few very effective bits of business than when he uses a great many, even though the many may be carefully worked out and thoroughly in keeping with the person presented. The audience is able to perceive and remember the few, associating them with the character, but the many simply create a confused impression. In directing inexperienced actors the director will find that they always want to be doing something; they are unhappy and ill at ease if expected to remain any time on the stage with nothing to do or say. One of his most difficult jobs will be to teach them to stand still, to listen and to stay in character when they have nothing to do.

There are three fundamental phases of action that an actor uses in characterizing through business. They are gesture, attitude and bearing.

Gesture. Gesture may be broadly defined as "an expressive" bodily movement. It is usually a movement of the arms, hands or head. Gestures are usually made in response to some definite and momentary stimulus and are an expression of transitory thought or feeling. For this reason they are a more superficial and less deeply rooted expression of character than either attitude or bearing.

Mannerisms are gestures that have become so habitual that they are used unconsciously and without immediate stimulus. If traced back such mannerisms will be found to have originated in a gesture in response to transitory stimulus. If a woman habitually makes the gesture of smoothing back the hair from her forehead with no apparent reason, it is probable that as a child she wore her hair in such a way that it was apt to get into her eyes.

Mannerisms are an excellent means of developing character parts. They should be used sparingly and with care in straight parts. The director must also check the use of mannerisms characteristic of the actor and not the character, a difficult matter as the actor will not realize his use of them.

Hands are one of the most valuable and vital parts of an actor's physical equipment. Many of the great actors have been famous for the expressive use of their hands. Certainly they are capable of more emotional expression than any other single part of the body except the face. They are, moreover, a very noticeable part of the body, and unfortunately one which the inexperienced actor seems to have the least imagination about. The director should encourage his actors to use their hands consciously, to know what the character would be likely to do with his hands. By doing so he forestalls the ubiquitous thrusting of hands into pockets and the hopeless question, "What shall I do with my hands?" In an attempt to "use his hands" the inexperienced player will often develop one or two gestures and use them constantly. Even though the gestures may have been good to start with their constant use will take all meaning from them. The actor must work for variety.

Attitude. Attitude is a significant and expressive position of the body or part of it that indicates the physical or emotional condition of the character. A man may walk with bowed shoulders under the influence of sorrow who habitually carries himself erect. Attitude is, therefore, also an expression of passing thought or emotion, but the stimulus is less transitory than for gesture and may affect the character more deeply. Partly because attitude is usually a response to something more fundamental than the stimulus that produces gesture and partly because the attitude that results from the stimulus varies more with different characters, it is a more accurate means of delineation of character. The relaxed attitude, expressive of weariness, will be decidedly different as used by a "dowager" and a young girl, whereas they may both use the same gesture of the head to express negation. As far as the character is concerned attitude may be either conscious or unconscious; it should never be unconscious on the part of the actor.

Bearing. Of the three phases, bearing is the most deeply rooted and, since it is unconscious on the part of the character, significant. It comes out of the conditions and habits of the character's life both physical and mental. The bearing of very small children is similar, unless the element of ill health enters in. Before they are very far along in years, however, such characteristics as shyness, vivacity, selfishness, etc. begin to develop, all more or less influencing the bearing of the individual child. By the time adolescence is reached the differences in bearing will become marked and will indicate fairly accurately the type of person the individual is. The physical conditions of life have perhaps a more direct and simple effect on bearing than mental qualities. The slow and plodding walk and bowed shoulders of the life-long farmer will stand out in contrast to the alert bearing and brisk movements of the city business man. A worker in a factory will show in his bearing the effects of hard labor, but they will not be the same effects as those shown by the farmer. Bearing involves the use of the whole body. The actor whose body is flexible and under control can use it to create character just as fully and effectively as he uses his voice.

Manners. The question of "manners" on the stage is largely a matter of period, locale and the individual character's background and up-bringing. It will enter into the use of business to a great extent. In this casual and easy-going age there are many things that we do in everyday life which should be avoided as business unless they definitely contribute to character portrayal. If the director will remember that nothing should be done in the production of a play that does not have some definite reason or intention behind it, and that the stage often gives importance to actions that are very casual and trivial in daily life, his own judgment and taste will tell him what to eliminate. The director should also recognize the fact that there is no absolute standard of good manners; that they vary slightly in different regions. For instance, the custom of shaking hands is much more prevalent in some parts of this country than in others. Unless the play is set in some very definite environment, where the audience expect to see manners that differ from their own, the director is safe in adhering to the manners of his own region. They will pass unnoticed and unquestioned, where manners that conformed to the actual locality of the play might arouse question and comment and thus draw far too much attention to themselves. When George Arliss played "Old English" in this country, people who were unfamiliar with the English custom of handling knife and fork accused him of showing bad table manners, and were unable to understand their use in connection with the character he played.

Business Used for Technical Purposes

The director may invent business for any one of three purely technical reasons: to help break up a conversational scene, to aid in building a climax, or for comedy purposes.

For Breaking up. When an author has written a scene in which people do nothing but talk the director must put his imagination to work to invent something for them to do. This is particularly true in scenes near the opening of the play, before the audience has had time to become interested in story or people. But even when plot interest is well developed, the audience wants to see something as well as to hear something. It is only when the interest in what is to come out of the dialogue is very tense that the director can eliminate business entirely. In such scenes, having great suspense value, business should be minimized as much as possible since far from adding to the interest it may only prove distracting.

When business is created for this technical reason it must be carefully selected and motivated so that its technical purpose will not be obvious. It can often be made to help create atmosphere, and it must always be in character for the actor to whom it is given.

For Building a Climax. In scenes of increasing tension, business that is indicative of the mounting emotions will be helpful in creating the desired response. It should usually increase in amount and importance as the scene progresses. Sometimes it may be the motivation for sounds which also help to build the climax, as when an angry man bangs his fist on the table.

For Comedy Purposes. In farce and low comedy, the director can often invent business, either to accompany the dialogue or separate from it, that is funny in itself and adds to the gaiety of the occasion. Such business may be anything from the slap-stick of farce to clever mannerisms in a character comedy.

But business that is not in itself funny may be used for the purpose of pointing laugh lines in all forms of comedy. A piece of business, often as slight as the lifting of an eye-brow, inserted just before the laugh-provoking phrase, will help to set it off and give it emphasis. Business may also be effectively inserted after a laugh line to motivate a pause and give a chance for the laugh to grow. Such business also serves to maintain the rhythm of the play when the laugh fails. The use of business for this purpose is particularly desirable in connection with sporadic laugh lines in a serious play. The rhythm in which comedy is written usually allows for laughter.

CHAPTER VI

THE STAGE PICTURE

As an audience watches a play it looks at a series of pictures, constantly changing and blending from one into another. The director's planning of these pictures will involve the consideration of two elements, the first, composition of the stage picture, the second, expression of the dramatic situation of the scene.

In designing the living pictures presented on the stage, the director makes use of the elements used in any of the graphic arts, such as emphasis, proportion, balance, variety, harmony and grace, and these elements must be applied both to the individual actor and the group. Of course stage pictures more often involve a group than a single actor, but the physical pictures presented by the individuals that make up the group are the elements out of which the whole design is fabricated.

THE INDIVIDUAL ACTOR

The individual actor in the stage picture must be considered in relation to the audience, the setting and properties, and the other actors.

The Actor in Relation to the Audience. An actor may assume any number of positions in relation to the audience from facing them directly to turning his back on them. For purposes of discussion, however, we can limit the number to five, namely, full face to audience, three quarter face to audience, half round or profile to audience, full back to audience and three quarters back to audience. They have been named in the order of their strength, the strongest first.

In discussing these positions the terms strong and weak will be used, as in the case of areas, simply to denote the relative attention value of the positions and not to suggest desirable or undesirable, effective or ineffective. For instance, the position full face to audience is the strongest, the one with most attention value. It is the position taken by a public speaker, just as the down center area on the platform is the area used by him. Both area and position are difficult to use in dramatic productions.

The position full face to audience, unless it is carefully motivated is apt to give the actor too direct a relationship with the audience so that they feel that he is speaking to them rather than to the other characters. It is possible to use it effectively from the up center area for a thoughtful "to himself" speech when the actor would not be expected to look toward the other characters, but use it sparingly and carefully even for soliloquy. It is almost impossible to use it from the down stage areas in a play that aims at naturalism. These suggestions of course do not apply to a play given definitely in the style of one of the artificial periods of the theatre when it was customary for the actors to address the audience directly, nor for one produced in a highly expressionistic or stylized manner.

If the director feels that it is necessary for a certain line to be given directly out toward the audience and yet wishes to keep such delivery unobtrusive and natural, he must plan for it in his business. The actor who is to speak the line may be turned away from the person with whom he is playing by some bit of business, such as looking out a door or window, flicking ashes from his cigarette into a fireplace—anything will do that can be adequately motivated and is not too interesting in itself. His attention is then drawn back by a speech from the other actor. With his back still to the other actor, he turns his head and gives the important line over his shoulder, thus having his full face to the audience, without the position being either hard or unnatural.

The position three quarters toward the audience, when used from an up stage area, relates the actor fairly directly to the audience, but at the same time enables him to assume a bodily relationship with other actors in the down stage areas. When used in the down stage areas this position is apt to appear hard and unnatural and it usually seems artificial, also, if the actor using it is playing a scene with another actor on a level with him. In other words it needs to be motivated, at least in a realistic play, by actors further down stage, toward which the actor in question is apparently turned.

The profile position is one of general utility. It may be used at any level from the curtain line without appearing unnatural, and it gives the actor sufficient relationship to the audience without impairing his rela-

tionship with the setting or other characters on the
stage. An actor playing in this position can open-up
slightly, that is strengthen his position with relation to
the audience, by standing with his up stage foot forward.

Because of the direct relationship expressed the position of back to the audience is stronger than three quarters turned away. In fact, considered purely pictorially,
it may even be said to be stronger than any position
except that of full face. The director however can sel-
dom separate so entirely the picture and the dialogue
and the more directly an actor turns his face to the
audience the easier it is for him to project and the audience to hear the lines.

The three quarters turned away position is usually
used from the down stage areas and by the less important characters in the scene.

The Actor in Relation to the Setting. The setting
is the background of the picture presented by the actors
and each individual must have as direct a relationship
to it as the figures in a painting have to the background
of the painting. The fact that the relationship changes
from moment to moment only intensifies the need for
careful consideration of it.

The size and shape of the various elements of the
setting, its lines and color, will all have some effect on
the actor. For example, a large and imposing window
may serve to dwarf, and thereby minimize the importance of an actor approaching it too directly or closely;
a large and important chair close to which he stands
may serve to give him pictorial importance.

These things will be instinctively felt by the director who has or who develops a keen sense of design.

If an actor is not a vital part of the scene in progress he will probably be withdrawn from the other actors on the stage and turned away from them. This will intensify his relation to the set and needs careful consideration. If he turns away directly toward a solid blank wall his position seems artificial. It is far more natural if he appears to be looking from a window or door or even down into a fireplace though there may be no fire there. We do not usually, even when deep in thought, stand directly facing a blank wall.

The actor's relation to furniture has been discussed in a preceding chapter. The director must remember that when an actor comes close to any piece of furniture the audience sees him and the piece of furniture not as separate units in the picture but as one unit, as in the case of the chair mentioned above.

The Actor in Relation to Other Actors. When two actors play a scene together the scene is one of two types, depending on whether the characters are of equal importance or whether one is of more importance than the other. If the characters are equally important, that is, if both have important lines or business, the scene is said to be "shared." In such a scene the actors play on a level with each other and their positions will be either three quarters face to audience or profile. The latter positions are more natural and direct and are advisable in a realistic play, especially if the scene has tension. (Not more than two actors should play on a level. It is a common fault of the inexperienced director to allow

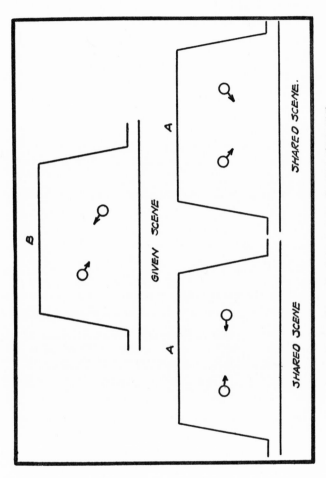

DIAGRAM V — SHARED AND GIVEN SCENES.

the actors to stand in a straight line.) If on the other hand, the scene has definitely shown itself as belonging to only one of the characters, if he has the important lines and business, then the scene is said to be "given" to him and he "takes stage" of the other actor. The important actor's position will be three quarters face to audience, that of the other actor three quarters back to audience. (Diagram V)

In a scene among a group of actors the same rule of putting the more important actor or actors up stage holds, since that enables the bodily position of the actor or actors to be related directly not only to the people with whom they are playing but to the audience as well.

Variety. The director must work for variety in the positions of his individual actors; that is they must differ from each other when they are part of a group and no individual should keep his position unchanged too long. This is especially important in long scenes where there is little movement or business required. Changes in the picture presented by the individual actor may be made by slight movements or shifting of the bodily position. Such changes must be timed so that the design of the group as a whole is not destroyed.

When, however, the actor is outside the scene, that is, not a part of the center of interest, it is advisable for him to hold a static position. The picture he presents will not become tiresome since the audience will be only vaguely aware of him, and any change or movement on his part may draw attention to him that should be kept with the other characters.

The Group Picture

The director uses the principles of graphic composition much more directly in designing the picture presented by a group than that presented by the single actor. A close study of the great masterpieces of painting in which many human figures are portrayed will afford suggestions for groupings that embody these principles. In addition the stage picture must have the variety of almost constant change without sacrificing any of the other elements.

Perhaps the two most important principles of composition from the director's point of view will be found to be balance and emphasis.

Balance. There are many elements that enter into balance: size, color, mass, weight and, most important for the director, interest. Two things of the same size may for instance balance each other as long as they are of the same color, but if one is decidedly darker or brighter than the other the balance may be destroyed. Thus the costumes of the actors must be considered as an element in the balance of the stage picture. Two actors well down stage will over-balance a larger group up stage, since they, being closer the audience, seem like a larger mass. As the artist who paints a picture may balance a large area of blank sky with a small area of landscape filled with detail, so may the director balance a large group of unimportant characters by one or two in whom the audience has much interest. Romeo meeting Juliet for the first time in the fifth scene of the first act has so much more interest for the audience than all the rest of Capulet's many guests, that those two figures placed at one side of the stage balance all the gaiety and confusion of the party assembled on the other. Aside from the dramatic interest of the character, an actor can be given a fortuitous interest by placing him in a strong area or bodily position, or by giving him some attention-attracting business that will serve to create a balance between his single figure and a group.

A symmetrical grouping or arrangement of characters is an ineffective way to secure balance unless the scene is one of great formality, as courtiers on each side of a throne, or unless the director is using the old farce technique in directing that type of play, or deliberately achieving some effect of stylization. It is less obvious to obtain your balance through the use of some of the other elements mentioned than to depend on mere numbers for it.

Stability. In order to secure balance in a scene in which large numbers of people appear, it is necessary to keep some of the characters close to the edges of the picture. That is, if your center of interest and most of your characters are up stage, it will be found necessary in order to give the picture stability to have some people kept in the corners down right and left. The larger the group up center the more individuals you will need down right and left to stabilize your picture. No matter how natural it would be for everyone on stage to crowd to the center of interest, you must find reasons for holding some of them at the sides, for the minute the sides of the stage become empty, the picture you present to the audience is unbalanced.

Balance is a more difficult problem for the director than for the painter since the director's picture is constantly changing. The Movements for Compensation are one means the director uses to maintain balance as his picture changes.

Emphasis. A picture, every part of which was just as interesting as every other part, would be a monotone. Since, as we will see when we consider the visual presentation of the dramatic situation of the scene, the stage picture must be closely related to the story, emphasis is an even more important element in it than in a painting. Certain characters must be drawn to the attention of the audience in each scene; they must be emphasized.

A character may be made to stand out pictorially from other characters on the stage by being placed in an area that is either arbitrarily stronger or has been made so by the use of a higher floor. He may be made more important by being placed in a closer relationship with the audience through facing them more directly. Or he may be emphasized by the use of focus, space or reinforcement.

Focus. Focus is the arrangement of the various elements in the picture in such a way as to lead the eyes and the attention of the audience to one point. The grouping of the characters in a straight line with the important character at the up stage end is a means of focusing attention on him. The arrangement of actors in the form of a triangle—it need not, indeed, usually should not, be an equilateral triangle—with the important person at the apex is perhaps a more effective use

of focus. Either of the arrangements described above
will serve to direct the attention to the person to be
emphasized, but they will be more effective if the actors
in the group are placed so that they will look toward
the important person. Indeed, a "visual focus," that is,
having all the characters on the stage look at the person
to be emphasized, is frequently just as effective as the
use of line or triangle.

The use of focus in a scene involving a great many
characters can be given variety and kept from becoming obvious by the use of counter focus in the smaller
groups. (Diagram VI) That is the people in the small
group can focus directly on one of their group who in
turn will focus directly on the center of interest. Such
counter focus, far from distracting from the main focus, serves to strengthen it by adding interest.

Space. An important character can often be emphasized by being kept to himself. If he is placed farther
from the other characters than they are from each other
he will be more prominent.

Reinforcement. A character followed or backed by
a group will gain increased importance, as a general
followed by troops. A man standing by a chair will be
pictorially more important than if he stood alone. In
the first instance there should be space between the
actor and the group, enough so that the important character does not become just one of many but not enough
to make him a separate unit from the group or the increase in weight is lost. In the case of the chair the
actor should stand close to it, since he will not become

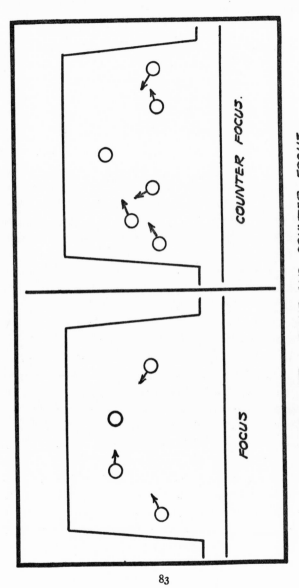

COUNTER FOCUS.

FOCUS

DIAGRAM VI — FOCUS AND COUNTER FOCUS.

identified with it and the closer he stands the more unified and important the two become.

VISUAL PRESENTATION OF THE DRAMATIC SITUATION

The director should endeavor to design his stage picture so that each scene of the play will have at least some meaning for a deaf person. That is, the situations as they develop should be illustrated by the grouping of the actors and their individual bodily positions. Character relationships and individual reactions indicated in the lines of the play become more clear and emphatic to the audience when they are thus pictured.

The positions of a group of actors should, therefore, never be casual or accidental; nor should they be merely beautiful; they should be carefully designed to strengthen the values of the scene. The grouping and individual positions selected to picture the meaning of the scene will be influenced by the social standing and environment of the characters, by the conventions they recognize and by other factors just as verbal expression of emotion is influenced by such factors.

The picturization of the individual's emotional state is usually a matter of business; it has been discussed under gesture and attitude.

When the director has reserved a certain area to stand for a certain idea or character, he may picture the meaning of the scene by grouping his characters with relation to that area; those in sympathy in or close to the area, those in opposition withdrawn from it. Certain pieces of furniture have naturally or can be given by careful pointing definite associations that make them valuable aids in picturing a scene. An elaborate high-backed chair has a certain throne-like quality that suggests authority. It is used throughout many scenes as the seat of a dominating old man. But the time comes when his granddaughter takes the power out of his hands. The old man no longer sits in the chair; it becomes the girl's seat and the other characters will be grouped about it at all times in relation to the part they take in the theme of authority.

Character Relationships. The most important element in graphically illustrating the story through stage pictures is that of character relationships. All character relationships fall under one of three general heads. The relationship is one of conflict, or it is one of sympathy or it is one of indifference, and the grouping of the characters must show us not only which relationship is involved but also the degree of feeling behind it.

Strong emotion, whether anger or love seems to draw people close together. Fear is the one emotion that separates them. Conflict therefore as well as love may be picturized with the characters in the same area. Conflict between two people appears more definite if they face each other across some piece of furniture, the chair or table graphically representing the barrier of misunderstanding between them. The actual physical barrier that it presents suggests subconsciously to the audience that if it were not there the conflict of words might become one of blows.

Many inexperienced actors seem to find turning their backs on the people they are playing with an easy

means of picturing all emotions from mere embarrassment to violent hate. The position does suggest conflict,
but it is to be avoided for three reasons: it makes the
scene artificial and difficult for the other actor, it is too
obvious, and it is too easy. If you ask the actor to portray his emotion in some other way he will have to work
harder and it is ten to one that the result will be more
effective.

In a scene of conflict in which a group of people is
involved, the two opposing forces may be lined up on
opposite sides of the stage. Care must be used that such
a grouping does not become too obvious. Counter focus
used within the separate groups will sometimes prevent
the grouping from being obvious, or one or two of the
less vitally concerned characters can be placed with the
opposing party. When this is done it is well to place
them in a weak area.

Sympathetic relationships are indicated by a close
approach and the use of one area. Usually only a small
number of characters are involved in such a scene. We
have covered the picturing of such scenes in detail in
the section dealing with Business for Love Scenes.

A relationship based on indifference is usually pictured by using different and distant areas for the characters. If two actors playing a scene together on the
same level both assume a position three quarters turned
to audience, they are apt to look indifferent to one another. The director should watch his actors that they
do not assume these positions when indifference is the
last thing that they want to illustrate!

CHAPTER VII

DIALOGUE

If the director will analyze any play he will find in it two distinct elements. The ratio in which they appear will vary greatly according to the type of play, but both will be present in some degree. These two elements are exposition and action. Exposition is the presentation of facts, frequently past facts, which account for situations and character relationships which the audience must comprehend, that prepare for or explain the action or that bridge gaps in it. Action is the progress of the drama as it is presented to the audience. It need not, of course, be physical action; it may be the psychological growth or change of the characters, it may be emotional developments, or it may combine any or all of these elements. Both exposition and action are necessary and they are usually handled by the author in separate scenes, though such a division is not necessary. Ibsen, for instance, was a master of delayed exposition that he used as a vital part of his action. Playwrights without his facility, however, find it easier or more convenient to handle them more or less in separate scenes in order that the action will not blur the exposition, nor the exposition clog the action.

We have, therefore, in most plays, Expository or

Static Scenes and Scenes of Action or Climax. The written dialogue will usually vary with the type of scene; certainly the director's treatment of it will be different.

EXPOSITORY OR STATIC SCENES

Expository scenes occur most frequently at the opening of a play, but they are also to be found all through the course of a play up to the very close. Mystery plays are apt to be heavily weighted with exposition right at the close when the how and why of who killed Cock Robin is finally explained to the audience. The occurrence of something vital to the plot, a time lapse between the acts—there are many things that may make it necessary for the author to stop his action in order to explain facts to the audience.

Expository scenes are usually scenes of dialogue with little or no action called for by the author. When they occur, as they most frequently do at the opening of a play, they occur before any element of conflict has been introduced and before the audience has had a chance to become interested in, or even to know, the characters. Often the very facts presented are not in themselves interesting, yet it is important that the audience comprehend them if they are to understand and follow the play. Therefore, in order to capture the interest of the audience and to hold their attention, the director must use all the technical means at his command.

Business. The first, easiest and most effective means to this end is business. Sometimes the author will suggest business. but director and actor can usually amplify it. Business for atmosphere and especially business for character are desirable since your audience is just getting acquainted with place and people.

Movement. Movement is also an excellent means for making the audience feel that something is happening. Remember, however, that by movement it is very easy to distract the attention of the audience from what is being said. And since the expository scene was written that certain facts in the dialogue might be heard, whatever movement is used must be so timed as not to blur those lines. The same is true, of course, with regard to business, though the danger is not so great. Small movements are frequently sufficient to give the scene the variety that will make it interesting. The imposed movement in such a scene is apt to increase and quicken as the drama begins to emerge until it blends into the necessary movement required by the story.

Stage Pictures. The director should give special thought to his stage pictures throughout an expository scene. If they are well designed the audience will enjoy looking at them and their attention will be held until an interest in the people and the story supplants it. The picture, however pleasing, must not be held static throughout a long scene; a new picture will often draw attention back to the stage when it might otherwise wander. In designing the stage pictures careful thought must also be given to the graphic illustration of character relationships. If the audience can see as well as hear that John is Mary's real son and Harry only her step-son, the fact will be planted more than twice as firmly in their minds.

Tempo and Rhythm. Tempo and rhythm will be found valuable aids in any static scene. The former may be quick, but should never be quick enough to seem hurried. A steady, rhythmic beat, consistently maintained will do far more to keep a static scene from dragging than a fast tempo. Such scenes should have an easy flow and the director must watch that the actors in a praiseworthy attempt to capture and hold the attention do not over-act. The expository plot lines must be carefully emphasized, but not "plugged." The audience is apt to resent over-playing or too obvious emphasis as a slur on its intelligence.

Transitional Scenes. Sometimes an author places a scene of dialogue without action between two scenes of action or climaxes in order to arouse suspense. The scene itself is quiet without any suspense element in the lines but it delays the action which the audience knows or fears or hopes is coming, thus increasing the anticipation. Such a scene may not be expository in the material presented, but it is static and should be handled with the same technique as an expository scene.

ACTION SCENES

The story of a play is presented to the audience through a series of action scenes, each of which builds to a point of greater interest or tension than the opening of the scene. This point or climax usually becomes higher and higher with each succeeding scene until the climax of the play itself is reached. The most difficult and important thing in directing a climactic scene is to

start it low enough to allow sufficient building before
the climax is reached and to retard the building so it
reaches its peak at the climactic point of the scene and
not before.

The director must keep constantly in mind all through
the earlier portions of the play that such climaxes as
occur must be topped as the climax of the play itself
approaches.

Since playwrights do not always produce perfect
scripts, the director as he works with his play is apt to
find that the climax of the first act, we will say, is one
of such power, or can easily be made so, that it naturally tops those of the succeeding acts. Shall he retain
the bird in hand, hoping thereby to make sure of his
audience, or shall he let it go with the intent of captur-
ing the two in the bush? It is a question of judgment,
but the more interested and excited the audience is by
the first act the more it expects of the succeeding two.
And it is the impression that exists in the mind of the
audience at the close of the play that it takes away with
it. It is usually better, therefore, deliberately to pull
down the earlier climax of the play that it may build in
a steadily mounting curve to its own main climax.

Not that any play will build steadily to such a climax.
Each minor climax will be followed by a drop, sometimes a descending scene, sometimes a decided drop
such as that made by an entrance or an exit, sometimes
by a static scene involving a different set of characters,
and sometimes by a pause of greater or less extent. The
entre-act intermissions are usually such pauses. After
one of these breaks the action will begin to mount

again. It will start probably from a point not quite as low as that at the opening of the preceding climactic scene, but considerably lower than its peak, and it will build to the next climax which will be at least slightly higher than the preceding one.

The Technique of Climax Building. There are many elements that may be used by the director in building a climax. Which ones he selects and how he treats them will depend on the dramatic values inherent in the scene.

Movement. Movement accompanying the dialogue is a very effective means of building climax, but it may be used in two opposite ways. The scene may start quietly and increase in amount, frequency, size and speed of movement or it may start with much movement and gradually drop to dead quiet. If the scene is one of physical action the former process will probably be indicated, if it is one of psychological interest it may well be the latter.

Dialogue. The speeches in a climactic scene will increase in intensity and volume, become quicker in tempo and be raised in pitch as the scene progresses. Not all these means will probably be used by the same characters, at least to the same degree. The ones selected will be chosen to suit the character and the type of scene.

The difference of one speech over the preceding one will usually be gauged from the beginning of each speech. That is the second speech will begin with greater intensity than that with which the one preceding it began. When a speech begins as high or higher than the preceding one ends, it is called "topping." Topping is effective used at the peak of the climax; it cannot be used in a scene of any length or the actors quickly reach a point beyond which they have no power to go.

A sharp attack and definite, quick response to cues, valuable as it is in almost any type of play, is especially necessary in mounting scenes. In certain instances the director may achieve a climax by instructing his actors to overlap slightly, that is, each actor to begin his speech before the preceding speech is quite finished. This of course is apt to blur the sense of the speech and even the feeling of intensity and excitement it creates does not compensate for the loss of clarity where important lines are concerned.

Sometimes a director feels that the author is taking too long to reach the climax of his scene, that his lines are unimportant and perhaps even repetitious. In such a case he can do better than overlap them, he can telescope them. That is, he can have two or more actors take the same cue and say their lines simultaneously. Occasionally you will find such a process indicated by the author; not frequently, however, as most playwrights prefer to have their lines heard. The director should remember the author's rights in this connection and use this means of building a climax only when he is sure that the tumult and the shouting are of greater value than what is being said. He should never try to continue telescoping too long. The audience, amused or thrilled at first, will soon become bored and impatient if they cannot hear the words. They have paid to hear and it is their right.

Technical Effects. The use of light and sound,

voices, music, etc., either on stage or off, will be found excellent means of building climax in scenes where they may legitimately be used. If they are unmotivated or incorrectly timed they may be simply distracting.

Extras. In mass dramas or scenes in which extras are used an increase in the number of people on the stage will help to create a sense of climax. To see the stage gradually filled as people come hurrying on, first singly, or in groups of two or three and then in larger numbers, with ever-increasing movement and sound, produces an unfailing, intense sense of excitement.

Areas. If, during the course of a climactic scene the action is moved from a weak area to a stronger one, the effect is good. If it moves from a strong area to a weak area, the director may wonder what has happened to his climax.

Scenes of Suspense. In addition to the two types of scenes, static and climactic, generally found, the director will sometimes come across a scene of pure suspense. The action does not advance, it does not build to a climax; it is simply held at a point of tension. In fact it frequently seems as though the author were trying to see how long he could keep his audience sitting breathless. There are frequently, in such a scene, slight rises or drops of intensity and the director must reinforce them, for the scene cannot be held very long at the same level without either snapping the attention of the audience or producing some undesired reaction, often laughter. If the director feels that such a scene as written is too long, that it cannot be held, then he should deliberately plan to drop the tension by a change in the tone or tempo with which the dialogue is spoken, or by some imposed movement or invented business. If he does this he must rebuild his scene, using any of the means suggested for the building of climaxes, back to its original point. The drop may be decided but it must be short.

EMPHASIS

A story put into dramatic form is compressed into two hours of telling and told to a large group of persons under conditions where distractions of all sorts are apt to occur. It is necessary, therefore, that the important elements both of action and of speech be "pointed up," so that the audience not only does not miss them, but also realizes that they are important to the story. The author has no time to amplify, he must emphasize; the director cannot explain, he must emphasize.

Indeed, the adjustment of emphasis all through the play, in all the various elements involved is the director's most important problem and duty. For emphasis is an appeal to the attention of the audience by the intensification of sense impressions, and the success of the production rests entirely on the success of that appeal.

We have discussed strong and weak areas, strong and weak movements, built entrances and pointed business, all explanatory of the use of emphasis in the physical elements of production. When we come to consider emphasis of speech, the subject becomes more complicated.

English is an inflected language, so that we will have minor and major emphasis occurring even in a very short speech. We cannot say two syllables in natural speech without stressing one of them more than the other. This form of emphasis, however, is one of the elements covered in a study of speech, and while every director must realize thoroughly its importance, the consideration of emphasis here will be limited to that which comes more directly into the province of the director.

Lines to be Emphasized. The only lines in a play that need emphasis, other than the inflectional emphasis mentioned above, are *plot* or *story lines*. The director who goes through his script carefully before he holds his first reading and not only marks such plot lines but decides on what means he wants to use to emphasize them will be rewarded with a production that is remarkable for clarity. His story will come out clearly and distinctly; and after all, the play was written and the production made in order that that particular story might be told. Plot lines will, of course, include the lines in expository scenes that give the audience facts that have preceded the opening of the play and that account for the situation and character relationships from which the play starts. They also include "plant" or "sign-posts" lines, lines that foreshadow something that is to happen later on, that may account for it, motivate it or at least keep the audience from feeling that it is unexpected or improbable.

If the idea or information contained in a plot line is repeated in other lines, the playwright has supplied much of the emphasis necessary. The director is safer, however, if he sees that the first mention of the idea or information is emphasized. Succeeding references will, once the audience has grasped the idea, serve to re-emphasize it without additional emphasis in the reading.

In reading comedy, "feeder" lines, that is, lines that without being funny themselves, supply the humor in a following speech, are generally emphasized. The only emphasis given the actual laugh lines is the inflectional emphasis referred to earlier in the chapter. Such emphasis must be subtly intensified to point a laugh line, but the line itself must never be "plugged." If it is, the audience is apt to get the idea that the character, or, even more probably and fatally, the actor thinks he is funny, an attitude which they quite rightly resent.

Methods of Emphasizing. The only method of emphasizing that the inexperienced actor knows, and one which all actors are apt to overwork, is increased projection. This method is good, and frequently useful and necessary, especially in scenes of mounting excitement, but there are others equally effective and less obvious. An increased intensity of tone will often secure the emphasis just as well as increased volume, or loudness. So will a sharp contrast in tone, such as the use of a decidedly higher or lower pitch, lifting or lightening the tone after intensity, etc. A whisper, following loud speech will give the secret spoken more emphasis than shouting it from the housetops. A marked change in tempo, whether slower or quicker, is also an excellent means of emphasizing.

The director's means of securing emphasis for important lines are not limited to the actor's reading of the line. Pauses are an excellent means of pointing important words, phrases and even entire speeches. The pause, carefully motivated of course, even if it is only slight arouses in the mind of the audience the unconscious question and anticipation of what is coming next. It may be motivated by the emotion of the speaker or by movement or business. If the business used is in close association with the idea to be emphasized the effect will be double in value. Emphasizing by gesture, the orator's method, may also be used by the actor. If the gesture comes simultaneously with the line it must reflect the idea of the line or else it will simply distract. If the gesture has no close association with the idea of the line, but is motivated in some other way, it should either precede or follow the line. Another means of emphasis similar to gesture but less "oratorical" is the stopping of an established movement, such as pacing up and down, knitting, etc., in order to speak the important line. It is not necessary that the movement be a big or important one.

If the speaker can be moved into an advantageous position in time for him to speak the important line, the line will be emphasized. A strong area, higher level, bright light or focus from other actors will give him the advantage necessary. A sharp change of focus directed toward an actor just before the important speech will serve to emphasize it without any change of position on his part.

The director can, of course, combine any of the above means when it seems desirable.

Softening. The director is apt to find lines in his play that he not only does not want to emphasize, but that he feels should be minimized. He may feel that they are out of character for the person who says them or that they are contrary to what he feels are the desirable dramatic values of the play. They may be lines that are awkwardly written or that have come to have a different significance today from that of the period in which they were written. In plays by less expert playwrights he may find an awkward bit of business or situation apologized for and thereby made more emphatic.

The question of cutting such lines is one of theatre ethics. In certain old plays they may be so treated, but, since the playwright has undoubted rights in the matter, it is usually safer, and just as effective, simply to soften them. Beside, they are often necessary to the progress of the dialogue, if not to the story. In this case the audience must of course hear them, but the director should do what he can to keep them as inconspicuous as possible.

What he can do is to soften the lines in one or more of the following ways. He can have them read in a quiet unobtrusive tone. This is called "throwing a line away." They should not be slurred or given with an indistinct enunciation. The minute the audience has any occasion to question in the least what it was the actor said, attention is called to the line and the director's purpose of having it heard without being noted is defeated. The speaker may be given business that will serve to distract the attention of the audience from what is being said; he may be placed in a weak area or playing position and in certain circumstances a counteracting picturization of idea may be used.

Sustained Sentences. A comma in the written script may indicate a definite pause, or, more probably, a breathing pause but it should never be marked by a drop of emphasis in the reading. If this is permitted the dialogue will have a jerky uneven effect and all easy flow will be destroyed. Inexperienced actors, and some not so inexperienced, are apt to drop the last words of a speech. In every day speech this is the natural thing to do. A dropped voice marks the end of a sentence. On the stage, however, the actor must learn to indicate the end of the sentence without an actual drop in emphasis. Even one actor with this fault can be responsible for dropping an entire scene. It is often a question of faulty breath control, too much breath being expended on the first part of the speech so that there is insufficient to give the last words their proper emphasis. In addition to the danger of dropping the scene, the actor must beware of such uneven emphasis since the idea of the speech is often contained in the last words of the sentence. For both these reasons the *last words of a speech must be as clearly emphasized as the first.*

Speech

The subject of speech is a very important one for the director, especially for the director working with untrained actors. The average voice is poorly placed and without full power; average diction and enunciation are slovenly and poor. The more the director knows of this subject the greater help he can be to his actors, but it is impossible for most people to change the speech habits of a lifetime in a six or eight week rehearsal period. The director, however, should ask them to try. The methods of teaching correct speech are almost as many as there are teachers. The writers make the following very general suggestions in the hope that they may be helpful during a short rehearsal period and with no claim whatever to have completely covered the subject.

The most vital speech problem and one that the director and actor will have to solve is that of projection. Resistence to fatigue is almost as important. Both are a matter of breathing correctly. The actor should be encouraged to develop his full lung capacity and to control the breath exhaled through speech so that he always has an adequate reserve.

In addition to the two points mentioned, the most important elements in good speech are good tone, good articulation and flexibility.

Good tone is largely a matter of resonance. The actor who shouts or forces his voice fails to attain resonance. He should work for an easy, open, relaxed utterance. The attempt to gain volume by use of a high pitch not only usually fails of its purpose, but is unpleasant in the result. Most voices are least pleasant in the upper half of their range. The actor should save his higher tones for special effects; also his lowest. The most pleasant pitch is usually lower than that in habitual use. A little experimentation should show the actor in which direction to try to expand his range.

Flexibility in voice gives the actor power to express the emotions and qualities conceived by his imagination. Only complete breath control, a wide range of pitch, and well developed resonance will give him a voice whose flexibility will meet the exacting requirements of his profession.

Perhaps one of the things that has been most injurious to the modern theatre in this country is the inaudibility of its actors. Many of them cannot be heard clearly and distinctly beyond the first few rows. The endeavor to achieve naturalness has been largely responsible for this serious error in our acting technique, but the gain in naturalistic playing has been bought too dearly by sacrifice of essential clarity.

Enunciation is the basis of clarity and clarity is a greatly prized quality in an actor. "I could understand every word he said" is a compliment that is paid to an actor usually with some feeling of surprise by the person extending the praise. Yet surely every actor should make the power to be understood his first objective. The proper placing of the voice makes for good enunciation. Swallowed words are never distinct. Correct vowel qualities and proper use of the lips in enunciating consonants are the fundamental elements necessary; the slurring or elision of letters, especially at the ends of words, is the greatest and most common fault. Special attention should be given to enunciation in plays using dialect or very colloquial dialogue.

Pronunciation should be a matter of normal English, acceptable everywhere. Localisms should be eliminated as far as possible and only such elements used as are nearly uniform everywhere. The director should have a good dictionary to act as referee in case of disputes.

Dialect. In producing a dialect play, the director has, in addition to all the usual problems, the responsibility of making the speech intelligible to the audience. By working into the dialect slowly, that is, by softening it in the opening scene, the ears of the audience have a chance to become adjusted to the unfamiliar sounds. The opening scenes will probably contain much exposition that it is important for the audience to understand, and it is better to sacrifice the local color of the speech than to risk having the audience lose information that it is necessary for them to have. When action has begun to take a more important part in the play, the dialect can be strengthened without the audience losing the thread of the story.

Speech rhythms, which are an important part of every dialect, can be used for their full value at all times. Actual word distortions, caused by the addition or elision of consonants or unusual vowel sounds should be used only after the audience has had a chance to accept the dialect. Especially careful attention must be given to the enunciation of such words as well as to other unfamiliar words and phrases.

In addition to making the dialect speech as clear as possible, the director can help the audience to follow the play by giving the plot lines additional emphasis and by making his stage picture express vividly the meaning of the scenes.

Vocal Interruptions. Scenes in which either laughing or crying occur will need careful rehearsing. They must be carefully timed that the sounds do not block the line, especially the actor's own lines. Yet the actor should not abruptly stop laughing or crying in order to speak. The interruption must be blended with the speech and a tone quality used that carries the idea of the interruption. In sobbing scenes when the face of the actor is hidden, care must be taken that the mouth is not covered. The eyes may be covered by the arm and the head turned with the face toward the audience. The director will often find it advisable to rehearse such scenes separately if his actors are inexperienced, until they have acquired confidence and mastered the technique.

Asides. Asides and soliloquies are not usually found in modern plays. If the director decides to do an old play in the modern manner, it is frequently better to cut such speeches where it is possible; if it is not possible they should be softened and read in a "covered," lower than natural, tone without very much emphasis, pantomime or facial expression. They are simply thought vocalized. In a period play directed in the style for which it was originally written, soliloquies and asides must be in keeping with the style selected. In such cases they are usually spoken to the audience.

CHAPTER VIII

THE ACTOR'S REACTION TO DIALOGUE

The director, especially when he works with inexperienced actors, should watch most carefully the player's work when he is not speaking. Many actors give good interpretations when they have something definite to do or say, but lose them the moment they become passive.

Continuity. If an actor can be led to think the character's thoughts, or at least to know what the character would be thinking, the entire time that he is on the stage, he is apt to remain in character. Such a thought continuity will, in addition to keeping the player always "in character" add to the richness of his characterization.

Listening. One of the most difficult things the actor has to learn is to listen imaginatively. He must hear what the other actor says and definitely suggest by his reaction that *he is hearing it for the first time*. His reaction to the speech will be, in most cases, twofold. Its significance will affect him directly but it will also make him want to say something in reply. It is the latter effect that will probably have the greatest influence on his reaction.

The simplest form of dialogue is that in which one

speech replies immediately and directly to the one preceding it. Such dialogue will usually be found in scenes where the emotional tension is great, in which the characters are intent on the subject under discussion. The actor's reactions will be comparatively simple. A scene of this sort is best played quietly and with little breaking up.

In scenes of a more casual nature, well written, natural dialogue will usually be more complex. Each character will be following his own trend of thought. Each speech will spring from the speaker's own thought continuity; it may be affected or colored by the dialogue immediately preceding, or it may spring with not much apparent connection from the character's individual reaction to the subject under discussion. It may even express an idea that has no relation to the subject of the dialogue that has preceded it. This sort of dialogue is often difficult to memorize, but if the actors involved in such a scene will each work out a thorough thought continuity for himself, memorization will be much easier. Not only will memorization be easier, but the reactions, otherwise difficult, will come naturally and effectively. Carefully planned business will help to unify such a scene and even in many cases to motivate or account for the apparently disconnected thoughts expressed in the speeches.

While listening an actor should look at the person speaking unless there is a definite purpose in having him look elsewhere, but his gaze should not be so intent as to become a fixed stare, nor should he always look directly into the eyes of the person with whom he is playing. A direct stare into the eyes may cause embarrassment or distraction. When the actor has a definite reason for looking somewhere else than at the person with whom he is playing, that somewhere else should not be the floor. Lowered eyelids, seen from the audience, give the actor an appearance of apathy, of lack of alertness and of being out of the scene, which is undesirable. If the character is apathetic, the actor can portray that characteristic by the use of his body. Many actors have a fondness for turning their backs on the person with whom they are playing, especially in emotional scenes or on speeches that suggest opposition. This means of picturization has been used so much that it has acquired artificiality. It is a too obvious picturization to be generally effective and it is apt to make it difficult for the other actor.

Cues. One of the commonest and most pernicious faults found in poorly directed productions is a slow and slovenly response to cues. Very often it is a matter of incorrect breathing which the director has not known how to correct. Unless there is a reason for a pause, the actor should attack his speech definitely and sharply the instant the preceding speech is finished. He should have his lungs full of air so that he does not even have to wait to inhale. Even an infinitesimal pause between speeches, a pause too slight to be perceived as such, will be felt by the audience. If such pauses occur to any extent, the tempo will be felt to be too slow, the scene will drop and the rhythm of the production will be destroyed. Especial care must naturally be used to secure a prompt response to the cue if the cue is a broken or interrupted speech. It is a good plan to have the actor giving the cue know beforehand what the rest of his speech would be and to continue speaking for a word or so if the actor who is supposed to interrupt does not respond to his cue promptly.

A thorough memorization is a necessary basis for the correct response to cues. The director who insists that his actors learn their lines early in the rehearsal period can devote his attention to this important factor in his production during the final rehearsals. It is impossible to check the timing of cues while the actors are still fumbling for, or even are the least bit uncertain of, their lines. The inexperienced actor when told to pick up his cues more quickly is apt to increase the tempo of his speech. This, of course, is not desirable, and the director must see that his actors understand the difference between a quick tempo and a quick response to cues.

The objection has been made that in natural speech people do not speak on cue. Most people, however, would rather talk than listen and in a general conversation they are apt to answer quickly to prevent someone else from speaking first. The stage interprets but does not reproduce life and it is not naturalness that makes a quick and accurate response desirable; it is the fact that the effect of a slow response to cues will lessen the emotional response the director desires from his audience.

Pauses. For variety and because the rhythm of the production will usually be found to demand it, definite pauses should be introduced by the director wherever they can be motivated. Pauses must however be carefully planned and timed. The emotion of the character, some piece of business or movement, a sound off-stage, etc. will motivate a pause. An unmotivated pause will give the feeling of forgotten lines. The length of the pause will depend on the situation. Actors vary in their ability to judge the correct length of a pause. If the actor is sensitive, the director can leave the matter safely in his hands. The length of the pause may vary from production to production with the actor's sensing of how deeply each particular audience is held. For the insensitive actor, and usually for the inexperienced one, it is safer for the director to give a definite count to regulate the length of time during which he is silent.

Telephone Conversations. A stage telephone conversation is a problem in the use of pauses. The pauses must be long enough to suggest the speech at the other end but not long enough to drop the interest of the audience. If the director will put the idea of what is being said by the other person into the fewest possible words and then instruct the actor to think those words during the pause, he will be apt to get the effect he wants. The actor will of course think them quicker than they could possibly be said, but the pause will seem to the waiting audience longer than it really is. Placing the actor so that the audience can see his face and giving him business with which to fill the pauses will also help greatly in holding the attention of the audience.

Overlapping. In scenes of excitement the usual response to cues may be varied by overlapping, that is, by having one speech begin a word or two before the preceding one ends. This procedure is discourteous to the other actor and should not be used except by the director's instruction to attain some definite dramatic effect.

Holding for Laughter. It is dangerous for a director to instruct a cast to wait for laughter on certain specified lines. Sometimes even a "sure fire" laugh line fails to get the laugh. Audiences vary greatly in what they find funny and an actor is not always equally expert in pointing his laugh lines. If the actors wait for laughter that fails to come the tempo and rhythm are spoiled and the scene drags. It is better to let your actors kill some of the laughs by quick responses to cues, yet that should be avoided if possible.

Caution the actors about holding for laughs if and when they come. Let them analyze the play and decide in their own minds what lines are apt to produce laughter so that they will not be entirely unprepared for it if it comes. Experienced actors will hold for laughter instinctively, but an inexperienced cast will need help from the director in dealing with it.

If the actor has started to speak and realizes that a laugh is starting he should cease speaking at once, even if he has already said three or four words. He should then wait quietly and without moving, for movement may kill a laugh almost as effectively as speech. When the laughter has passed its peak and is beginning to drop, but before it has entirely died away, the actor should begin his speech again. His attack should be definite, sharp and clear for he must recapture the attention of the audience which has been dispersed through laughter.

The actor should be made to realize the importance of this technique. It is definitely discourteous to kill another actor's laugh by speaking too soon, and is apt to be injurious to the production as a whole. Audiences like to laugh and when the lines are comic it is certainly their right.

If the director feels that there are certain lines in the play that are sure to produce laughter, he can help his cast by planning business to follow them which will motivate and fill a definite pause. Such business will maintain the rhythm and tempo whether the laughter comes or not. It is especially desirable to do this for sporadic laugh lines occurring in a serious play. The rhythm of comedy usually allows for laughter, whereas that of a serious play does not.

CHAPTER IX

CHARACTERIZATION

The director's and actor's approach to characterization is quite different. The director's approach is that of analysis; the actor's that of interpretation. The actor's characterization should be more intimate and vital than the director's. It is analysis given expression.

The director uses analysis of character as one of his most important means of interpreting the dramatic content of the play. In the beginning he will know the characters better than the cast will, but as each actor works on his part he will come to know it better, or at least in more detail, than the director. The very closeness of the actor to the part, however, acts as a deterrent in many cases to his clear perception of the character in relation to the play. The director must constantly check the characterization as it emerges to be sure that it is contributing to the fullest possible extent to the dramatic values of the play as a whole.

In the early stages of rehearsal, the director should work with the actor in sympathetic cooperation on the analysis of the character, determining its part in the play and the values to be got from it. When the director and actor are in accord on these points the actual interpretation should be left to the actor. In the case of inexperienced, untrained players, the director will, of course, have much work to do in teaching them the technical means of expression, but his help should be confined as much as possible to technical suggestions. The actor should not be expected to imitate the director either in action or line reading—the finest imitation usually has much less spontaneity, vitality, and reality than an original conception even though the latter may not be so well executed.

Relation of the Character to the Play. The interpretation of character will be found to rest on four things: the relation of the character to the play, the dialogue he has to speak, what other characters say about him, and what the author says about him. Of these his relationship to the play is the most fundamental. The lines he speaks may be emphasized or softened to bring out this relationship.

Each character in a play has been put there by the playwright for a definite technical purpose. He may serve other purposes as well, but there is always one main reason why he is in the cast.

He may be there, and most characters are, to carry on the story. It is important that all the story characters know just what their functions are for each character must be interpreted to fulfill his own particular function. If each actor knows the main reason for his character being in the play he is not apt to have trouble in keeping the character in perspective throughout the course of the play. If, for instance, he realizes that his purpose is simply expository or to function in the denouement, it enables him to keep his role properly subdued during the other scenes in the play.

Some characters will be found to have been introduced mainly for atmospheric or comedy values. If the actors of such roles understand fully that they are there for those purposes, it will help them to present characterizations that accomplish what the director desires without infringing on the story or taking interest that by rights belongs to the story characters.

In addition to his technical purposes, every character will function in expressing the dramatic value of the play. The actors will have less difficulty in creating characters to bring out these values if the director will analyze the play for them and take them into his confidence as to how he plans to interpret the play. As far as characterization is concerned the emotional values of the play will rest on character relationships. Once the actor fully understands what his technical purpose is and what emotional values the director wishes him to bring out, he will have no difficulty in assuming the correct relationship to the other people of the play.

Dialogue. All lines of the dialogue of a play were written for one or more of the following reasons. They may tell the story. They may create atmosphere, by suggesting a past time, a special place or race of people, or by creating a mood quality. They may be comedy lines. Some lines are also found that serve simply to characterize the person speaking them. Whatever their purpose, all lines should be characterizing lines; that is, they should contain ideas that the speaker would naturally express under the circumstances and they should be worded as that character would naturally speak.

Lines that serve most directly to characterize are lines expressive of the character's individual reaction to other characters or to events. The reservation of certain words or phrases for the use of a particular person serves to characterize him in much the same way as the use of mannerisms in his business. Occasionally an actor will have lines to speak descriptive of his own character and these, whether true or false, will give him an excellent clue to his character. Very important lines are lines that contribute directly to the dramatic values of the play since they serve to indicate his relationship to other characters.

In a poorly written play or in the case of very minor characters such as "the first waiter," etc., the actor frequently has to tax his imagination to create a character who might conceivably say the lines assigned to him. He must in such a case invent characteristics that will enable him to say the lines and make them sound real.

In addition to what he, himself, has to say the actor often finds important clues for the interpretation of his character in what other characters say about him. The actor should remember, however, that such speeches will be colored by the character of the speaker. They may be accurate descriptions, the antithesis of the truth or anything in between, so that it is the spirit behind them that the actor must consider rather than the mere statement. Whether true or false they afford accurate suggestions of the character relationships involved.

The Author's Descriptions. The amount of description supplied by the playwright may vary between a mere statement of relationship such as "his son," "his brother," etc., found applied to some of Shakespeare's characters, to whole paragraphs in the plays of Shaw and Barrie.

The author's descriptions may be purely objective, descriptions of appearance, manner, costume, etc., or they may be subjective analysis of the character's mental and emotional characteristics. The director should give consideration to the objective description in casting, but it is of course more satisfactory to use an actor capable of presenting the subjective characterization of the character than one who merely looks the part if the two qualities are not available in the same actor. The audience, unlike the playwright, has no preconceived idea of what the character looks like, and unless his appearance plays a definite part in the dramatic values of the play, they can be counted upon to accept the character's aspect without question.

The objective characterization must necessarily be made on the basis of the actor's body and voice and it is better for him to use them vividly and convincingly in his own way than to try to make them fit the author's description if they do not more or less naturally conform to it.

In a well written play a subjective analysis of the character should not be necessary; his characteristics should be apparent from a study of his place in the play and the lines he is given to say. When the author supplies such a description, however, it usually indicates to the actor what he must look for and emphasize in his relationship to the other characters and in his dialogue.

It is the director's privilege, in his endeavor to bring out what he considers the most effective dramatic values of the play, to emphasize certain of the character's characteristics and to soften or subdue others. In this way he may change the character's relationships to other people of the play so as to gain from the audience what he feels will be a greater emotional response. Such a change in character, however, must be purely a matter of emphasis; the director has no right to rewrite or cut lines. He must be careful that any change is a matter of interpretation and not an infringement of the author's rights. If there is a difference, the actor must accept the director's ideas for characterization rather than the author's.

Interpretation of Character. Character interpretation consists of two phases, the objective and the subjective.

Objective characterization is the presentation of the surface personality through the character's appearance and actions. This is the phase the actor usually conceives first, and early in the rehearsal period he will probably have quite definite ideas of what his make-up will be, in a general way what he will want to wear, etc. Of course as he progresses with his subjective characterization his ideas will change somewhat, at least they will acquire perfection of detail.

The character's appearance, as has been said, will depend on costume and make-up, but quite as much on bearing, posture and walk.

The actions of the character will also help to present him objectively. Attitudes, gestures, manners and mannerisms all help us to see the kind of person he is.

Subjective characterization comes slowly as the actor studies his role, for it is the presentation of the character's mental and emotional qualities. The mental qualities will be expressed largely in the way he reads his lines, by his manner of delivery, the emphasis and phrasing with which he gives his lines. Emotional qualities are also portrayed through speech by the use of tempo and tone quality, but the use of the body is also most important. Many actors, especially untrained actors, read their lines excellently but fail to use their bodies imaginatively in expressing emotion. An attitude or gesture may do as much to make the audience realize what the character is feeling and to arouse the proper response in them as the most emotionally delivered speech.

To create subjectively the actor must know imaginatively what the character's history has been, what his background is, what his activities and pursuits are, outside the frame of the play. The more the actor knows about him beside what the author has put into the play the richer his characterization will be.

When a character changes or develops during the play it is often advisable to rehearse the first and last scenes in juxtaposition so that the actor may have a vivid realization of the contrast he must create by slow degrees as the play progresses.

Both objectively and subjectively the actor who conceives clearly and presents accurately a limited number of characteristics usually presents a more vividly highlighted and clear-cut character than the actor who conceives and tries to portray all the characteristics that might naturally belong to his character.

Emotion. There are two halves to an actor's mind. One is occupied with himself, the actor. With this half he follows the technique of his art, gauges his pauses, governs his movements, makes adjustments, takes care of emergencies, etc. The other half becomes the character, thinks his thoughts, expresses his ideas, reacts to his emotions.

These two halves should be in nice adjustment. If the first prevails at the expense of the second the actor may give a technically satisfactory performance but it will probably be unreal and unconvincing. If the second prevails too greatly, his performance is apt to be uncertain and unreliable. It will frequently lack poise and finish.

For this reason the actor should beware of actually feeling too much emotion. He cannot "lose himself" in his role without danger of destroying the routine so carefully built up during rehearsal both for himself and the others.

The director will find that a vivid imagination, a keen sensibility and accurate response to other characters and to the environment presented are more satisfactory qualities in an actor than pure emotion. The ideal for an actor, as has frequently been said, should be "a warm heart and a cool head."

CHAPTER X

TEMPO, RHYTHM AND STYLE

In considering the production as a whole, we find that there are three essential qualities. They are entirely in the hands of the director and on their successful use will rest the worth of the production as an interpretive work of art. They are tempo, rhythm and style. The finish of the production will rest largely on the correct use of the first two, its unity and mood will be established by the last two.

Tempo. Tempo is the rate or speed of playing; it rests on the rapidity of movement and of speech and the quickness with which one thing follows another. Tempo varies continuously throughout the play; some scenes will be of a constant tempo, some will change in tempo. Especially in action scenes the tempo is apt to increase in speed throughout as a means of building the climax.

Each character in the play will have his own individual tempo as part of his characterization, but that tempo must remain relative to the tempo of the scene as a whole. Excitement, for instance, is apt to quicken speech and even a man who naturally speaks slowly will speak quicker when under its influence. Of course, his quicker speech may not be as quick as that of another character who is not excited. Sometimes the director will find it advisable to ask an actor to sacrifice that phase of his characterization in certain scenes in order that he may get the dramatic effect he wants from a more unified tempo. The actor in question can usually maintain his characterization by slightly increased emphasis on other factors.

A frequent fault with actors is a tendency to drop into a common tempo. This is especially true if some one member of the cast is using a very marked and decided tempo, either slower or faster than that of ordinary speech. This copying of tempo is entirely unconscious on the actor's part; it must be checked by the director when it first appears and corrected before it becomes set.

The establishing of tempo as a quality of his production is one of the last things the director works for. It is futile and distracting for him to pay any attention to it until the actors have thoroughly completed their memorization and the business used in the play is absolutely established. When these elements run smoothly the director can tell whether movements, line readings or cues need to be quickened or slowed down.

Rhythm. Rhythm is a much discussed subject and, at least as far as its use in the theatre goes, a complex one. The director should, of course, understand its meaning and use and know what effect the selection and maintenance of rhythm will have on his production, but he can usually leave its actual creation in the hands of his actors. This is just as true, or perhaps even more true, in the case of inexperienced players who have no idea that a dramatic production has rhythm, for rhythm is an element innate in all of us. Perhaps the fact that the functions of our bodies are rhythmical accounts for our unconscious perception of and quick response to rhythm.

The sensitive actor who is imaginatively aware of the atmosphere and characters of the play and familiar with the environment and characteristics presented, will instinctively and entirely subconsciously fall into a rhythm of playing that expresses those elements and establishes the correct mood quality for the play. Any interference or instruction on the part of the director is apt to make him self-conscious about the matter so that he loses the quality altogether.

It is only when the director has actors either ignorant of or insensitive to the general atmosphere necessary to the play, that he will have to establish the right rhythm for them. Sometimes there will be one member of the cast who fails to create the desired rhythm; if he cannot be led to fall into it after a few rehearsals, that role had better be recast. One such person can as thoroughly destroy the rhythm of a production as if it had never been established.

The correct rhythm of the production should begin to be apparent very early in the rehearsal period; at least there should be marked indications of it. Of course it will not be thoroughly maintained until later, but if it is not possible by the third or fourth rehearsal to distinguish the rhythmic beat of the play through a majority of the scenes, something is wrong and the director should take a hand. Unless he is dealing with thoroughly experienced actors, he will be wiser not to take the cast into his confidence. If they consciously work to establish a rhythm it is apt to be attained at the sacri-

fice of simple, natural playing, to be too strongly stressed
and hence to become obvious. Except in stylized or man-
nered productions this is undesirable, for the audience
should feel the rhythm without consciously perceiving
it. If the director feels that the rhythm is lacking or
wrong, he can usually establish or correct it without letting his cast know what he is doing by an expert manipu-
lation of emphasis on the various elements of the production.

For rhythm is based on the regular recurrence of emphasis.

Rhythm may be auditory as in music or poetry, it may
be visual as in the graphic arts, or it may combine both
as in the dance and the theatre.

Rhythm, whether auditory or visual, is established by
combining units into groups and accenting or emphasizing one of them. The individual rhythm will depend first
on the number of units in the group and second on the
placing of the accented unit. The number of unaccented
units in each group may vary without destroying the
rhythm, provided the variation is kept to multiples of the
original number and the ratio of unaccented units to one
accent remains constant. For example, a rhythm of two
unaccented units to one accented unit may be varied by
dividing each of the two unaccented beats in half, thus
having a measure in which there are four unaccented
units, each one of which is half the value of one of the
original two unaccented units. The rhythm is still the
same. If, however, in a group of three units the accent
is shifted from the last unit in the group to the first, a
different rhythm results. And there will be still a third

rhythm if the accent is placed on the middle unit of the group.

The units that make up the rhythmic pattern of a dramatic production include all the elements involved and the recurring accent may fall now on one element and now on another. It may be a visual accent, a matter of the area used, of movement or business, of the stage picture, of change in light, or it may be an auditory accent, a matter of speech or sound. The number of elements involved makes the deliberate planning of rhythm a complex matter, but it also enables the director to use comparatively simple rhythms without becoming obvious.

The visual and auditory rhythms of a dramatic production must be unified and the resulting rhythm must be maintained constantly throughout the production. If the rhythm is broken or changed during the production it will lack unity and the mood quality will be destroyed.

For the rhythm selected for any dramatic production will come out of two things. It must be typical of the background and characters presented and it must reflect the type of play.

The elements to be considered in connection with the background and characters are the natural speech rhythm as, for example, Irish dialect, and the physical movements and ways of doing things natural to the people of the play.

The element in the type of play that most greatly influences the rhythm is the number, arrangement, and spacing of climaxes. Farces, high comedies, folk dramas, chronicle or story plays, or tragedies—each type will make a distinct use of action scenes. Since the climax of each of these scenes is a point of emphasis, their arrangement will influence the rhythm used.

The audience response to rhythm is direct, though usually unconscious. Rhythm stimulates muscular action. Even when we repress the direct muscular response of clapping hands or stamping feet, the pattern persists in our bodies and creates an emotional reaction in us which we feel without consciously recognizing its source. The kind of emotion that will be aroused by a rhythm is largely a matter of association and may be different for each person. However, much of experience comes in the same form to all of us and our associations therefore are apt to be similar. A short, quick rhythm will pretty universally suggest a dance and gaiety, while a long, slow rhythm will be equally likely to suggest a funeral and gloom and sorrow. The director can count on and use rhythm to stimulate and unify an emotional response in the audience.

Since rhythm creates emotion its presence in long scenes of little action or dramatic tension is valuable in holding the audience. It can often be used, too, to make successful the production of a "dated" or otherwise unacceptable play.

In a stylized production other elements of the play are frequently subordinated to rhythm in an attempt to have it create a more intense and directly unified emotional response on the part of the audience. If the dramatic values of the play allow for this obvious use of rhythm, as, for instance, the mad nightmare quality of "The Emperor

Jones" most certainly does, the effect is splendid. The less obvious and more carefully subordinated use of rhythm in a more realistic type of production will if it is rightly selected and carefully maintained have almost as direct though far less conscious effect in arousing emotional response in the audience.

Style. Style in dramatic production, as in any work of art, consists in a unity of key that is in harmony with the subject presented. For a production to have style all its various elements must be in accord. To place realistic playing against an expressionistic background, using 18th century costumes, would be to lack style in the production as a whole, through an over-abundance of styles in its various phases.

The settings, costumes and manner of playing used in any production should all be governed by some element in the play itself, its type, its dramatic values, its period, or by the point of view with which the director approaches it. It seems essential, therefore, that the director should be responsible for all the factors that enter into the production. He should be what is known in Europe as a regisseur.

Productions in the American professional theatre often lack style owing to the fact that the producer and director are two different persons, the director being only one of a group of artists employed by the producer to "coach" the play and having no authority in any other field. In many instances he does not even select the cast. The players assembled may have been trained in various schools of acting, almost certainly they will not have played together as a group before. The style of acting in itself therefore often lacks unity, and it is only when the producer is a theatrical artist rather than the business manager that all the elements have the unity that creates style.

The style of a production may be given it through some close harmony of its various elements with its theme, as in an intensely rhythmic production of "Salome." It may acquire its style through careful and accurate presentation in the historical manner of the period in which it was written. Or the director may give it style through the individuality of his point of view. Of course there will always be much of this element in the work of any worthy director, for if one of the other methods of supplying style is used, it is the director who determines it. How far the point of view of the director may supplant the intention of the playwright is a matter of judgment. Perhaps it should depend on the relative worth of their imaginative powers. If the director feels that he has a play that is dull as it was originally conceived but that he can make interesting through the selection of some particular style other than that which the writer intended, he should be free to make the attempt. Max Reinhardt's production of "Midsummer Night's Dream" has been widely acclaimed but there are many people who feel that it was far more Reinhardt than Shakespeare, and there are even those who feel that in this instance the style supplied by the director did not show greater imaginative qualities than that innate in the play itself.

There are certain plays, such as those of Sheridan, written during a highly artificial period of the theatre, which seem to demand production in the artificial style in which they were conceived. They are charming when so given, but they have not the deeply fundamental humanity necessary for translation to another style. Sheridan's plays seem to be popular with little theatre groups, yet when they are attempted the production often falls below the standard of the group. This is because mere sincerity of playing will not carry them; they need on the part of both director and actors a thorough knowledge of their period and the style of playing which prevailed then.

Most of the great plays of the past, however, are great because they have a fundamental and universal appeal. Such plays are capable of being produced in many different styles. They may be given in their historic manner, they may be even "modernized" as when the plays of Shakespeare are presented in modern dress, or they may be given in a special style which the director feels illuminates anew their fundamental human theme.

There are, as the director will readily understand, an infinite number of styles possible in dramatic production. They range from extreme realism to the latest form of expressionistic presentation.

Realism. It is just as impossible to attain absolute realism on the stage as in any other form of art. The fourth wall of the room is always missing and the actors must use an unreal projection in order to be heard, to mention only two of the factors that make reality impossible.

It would not be desirable to strive for absolute realism even if it were possible to attain it, for all art is a matter of selection. The director who is producing a realistic play can, by careful selection of such realistic elements of setting, dress and action as best advance the dramatic content of the play, create in the minds of the audience the illusion of reality. Absolute reality, or as close an approach to it as it is possible to present, is apt to destroy its own purpose. The audience is made aware that they are looking at a stage through their wonder at the reality of the factors presented.

A realistic production can, and should, be made to express the inner meaning or dramatic content of the play by applying the same principles to everyday, matter of fact objects that the expressionist styles apply to whatever symbols they may use. A chair, well designed and correctly emphasized through direction, will stand for power just as adequately as any elevated perch onto which the director of the constructivist production may ask his actor to climb.

Expressionism. Expressionism in the theatre is an attempt to bring the abstract into the style of production. It is a reaction against representational or too literal presentations.

Beauty in abstract form is found in various degrees in all the arts, from Music, the most abstract, to Drama, the most concrete. Music has no specific or intellectual meaning; reaction to it is purely emotional. Drama on the other hand tells a definite and concrete story and depends for its reactions on the specific meaning of the dialogue and action. Drama as a whole therefore does not lend itself to abstract or symbolic treatment, though certain types of plays, the poetic, fantastic or symbolic, by their very nature are well adapted for its use.

Expressionism has a number of different phases, but the two most common are symbolism and stylization.

Symbolism. In this style certain characteristics of set and playing are exaggerated to symbolize certain qualities in the theme of the play.

Stylization. Stylization is the emphasis of any or all of the art principles of color, mass, line and form in order to create in the minds of the audience the desired emotional response.

Sense stimuli take on meaning only as they recall experience. Symbols and abstract qualities, therefore, may mean different things to different people unless they are such as are very common. Red and yellow are "warm" colors because they are associated with light or fire. Since light and fire are common experiences, we can count on a general reaction to them as "warm" colors.

The purpose of any work of art is to create an emotional response. Since the theatre, by its very nature, must arouse that response in a group, not an individual, it must, if it uses abstractions or symbols, choose such as can be counted on to create common reactions. If the symbol can be developed and given significance from its use in the production itself, the reaction to it will necessarily be unified. The use of an area to stand for a certain idea or quality is an instance of this type of symbolization. A realistic element may be made to stand for an abstract idea or symbol in this way just as readily and with as great significance as an expressionistic factor.

Constructivism. A great deal has been heard recently of the constructivist style. This style developed naturally in Russia and reflects the substitution of machines for man power with the consequent release of human energies for other purposes. It uses a mechanistic setting which has proved suitable for many of the propaganda plays which have formed so great a part of the recent Russian theatre. We may use this style in this country in the same way that we produce a play in the Chinese manner, as a curiosity or because of its educational interest. Without its native emotional background, however, it is very apt to seem like a mere affectation.

The director should consider carefully the dramatic values of the play before he decides on the style in which he will produce it. If he feels decidedly that these values will be better brought out by giving the production a style different from that which the author intended, it is his privilege as an artist to do so. The success of his production will depend on the quality of his judgment. If he accepts the style indicated by the script itself, his responsibility will be only for the success with which he uses it. Whatever style is used, selection, arrangement and the beauty of suitability are the essential elements that enable it to reflect the dramatic values of the play.

CHAPTER XI

THE DIRECTOR AND THE PLAY

When the director selects a play for production he has some definite reason for selecting that particular play rather than another. His reason may be purely adventitious, such as the fact that the play deals with a subject much in the public thoughts, that he has just the right actor for the leading role, that he needs that particular type of play to balance his program, that it is the sort of play which he can count on to balance his budget, etc. However, being an artist, the director is far more likely to select most of the plays he produces because they appeal to him personally and, even when he must choose a play for a utilitarian purpose, the range of available material is so great that he can usually find something that answers the need and yet appeals to him as an artist as well. As an interpretive artist he should have respect for the play he produces.

Having selected the play because it appeals to him, it becomes his function to present it to the audience in such a manner as will interpret for them the values that he finds in the play. In other words, he, as an interpretive artist, will present the play from his own personal point of view, which may or may not coincide with that of the author. There is usually more than one way of interpreting a great, or even a lesser, work of art, and it sometimes happens that the imagination of the interpretive artist will light upon values innate in it that were not apparent even to its creator.

The director then has the right to analyze the written play, to approach its production from whatever point of view he feels best reveals its dramatic content and to intensify certain elements and minimize others in order to gain for the production the maximum emotional value that his imagination can find in the written play. Such interpretation will be based, in the same way as is the actor's, on *emphasis*. The dramatic values must be innate in the play itself. The director simply brings them out; he cannot superimpose them. For instance, he should not cut, change or rewrite scenes and speeches in order to give the play a happy ending when it is obviously tragic in intent. The director's interpretation of dramatic values will rest on audience reaction. He will select for emphasis those elements in the play which his imagination tells him will create the greatest emotional response in the audience.

Emotional Response. Just what emotional response is and what produces it is a matter of psychology, and psychologists have written extensively on the subject. There are various schools of thought, and the matter is made more complex for the director because he is dealing with mass reactions and not the reactions of an individual. It is, however, pretty generally accepted that the responses to stimuli are of two kinds, those that affect us directly and cause direct reactions and those that affect us aesthetically and to which our responses are imitative. We touch with our fingers something hot and jerk our hand away. With this sort of direct response the director does not or should not have to deal. It is reality and the director is dealing with illusion.

Aesthetic Response. In contemplating a work of art the emotional response aroused in us is not direct; it is the reflection or duplication of the direct emotional response of the creator to the object or the idea he is presenting. When an actor shrinks back in fear, the audience experiences a reflex fear. It is an impersonal reaction which leaves them seated calmly in their seats. The cry of "fire" in a theatre has only too frequently aroused such a direct and personal reaction in the audience as has sent them on a mad stampede to the exits. It is this indirectness which constitutes "aesthetic distance" and creates the element of pleasure in our perception of emotions which if they were direct would be anything but pleasant.

Aesthetic Distance. In viewing a great work of art we become absorbed in it to the point of self-forgetfulness. This very self-forgetfulness constitutes the detachment necessary for aesthetic appreciation, for we are not self-forgetful in our reactions to daily living. When something in the work of art comes too close to us our reactions become direct and we are no longer self-forgetful. It is necessary therefore for the artist to create in his audience the subconscious feeling that what he looks upon is at a distance from him, not necessarily, of course, a physical distance, but rather a psychological or emotional distance that keeps his reaction to it abstract, indirect, impersonal.

The theatre, more than any other form of artistic

presentation, is basically realistic. It presents concrete visual images which are absent in the novel and poetry. It is three dimensional, which painting is not. It has animation and movement, lacking in sculpture and architecture. Its ideas and concepts are concrete while those of music are abstract. For these reasons the theatre is more real and comes closer to the audience than other art forms. It supplies stimuli to which emotional responses are more nearly direct. Recognizing this fact, the director must realize that the preservation of aesthetic distance in the theatre is most important and should be deliberately considered.

In spite of its fundamental reality there are, nevertheless, many elements in theatrical production that serve to create the desired aesthetic distance. It is established by such factors as the selection of certain objects and actions to create the illusion of reality and the elimination of others, the use of greater projection of voice and larger movements, gestures and even facial expressions on the part of the actor in order that he may "carry" to an audience at a distance, the opened up arrangement of setting and playing positions which indicate the absence of the fourth wall and the presence of the audience, the fact that ordinarily the actors move in light and the audience sits in darkness, and more important and fundamental than all, perhaps, the fact that the space allotted to the action of the play is distinct and different from that in which the audience sits.

Whenever any of these factors are changed or eliminated, whatever is gained by the change or elimination must be balanced against the resulting loss of aesthetic distance. To bring the action of the play down into the audience, for instance, will undoubtedly create a far greater intimacy, but the director must decide whether that intimacy with its consequent more direct and personal response is a better means of establishing the play's dramatic content than the maintenance of aesthetic distance by keeping the action in a distinct area.

The amount of aesthetic distance necessary to a dramatic production will vary greatly with the type of play. A psychological drama such as "Rosmersholm" or "John Gabriel Borkman" requires less than melodramas like "The Green Goddess." Our reactions to the former type of play are mental, and hence, by their nature, less direct and personal than the physical reactions aroused by the latter. As a rule stimuli productive of pleasant reactions require less aesthetic distance than those which arouse disagreeable responses. We are willing to be closer to pleasure than to pain.

The answer to the question of why people enjoy aesthetically emotional reactions which if they were felt directly might be exceedingly painful, lies in the fact that all emotional reactions whether direct or vicarious serve to broaden our experience. Because in the case of disagreeable emotions, such as sorrow or fear, this increased experience seems to cost too much, we welcome the chance to acquire them vicariously. Our pleasure rests on the feeling of increased knowledge and power brought to us through this added vicarious experience. Through it we become, as it were, omniscient.

The amount of aesthetic distance necessary to the production of any particular play will be determined by the point at which it ceases to *seem real* and *becomes real* to the audience. The illusion of reality in the theatre is based on a tacit agreement of the audience to enter into the pretense. "Let's pretend" say the playwright and the director when they raise the curtain and if play and production are at all adequate the audience is very ready and eager to do their part. When, however, something in the production comes too close to them they are jerked back out of their "let's pretend" attitude, become themselves seated in a theatre watching a play, and the illusion of reality disappears before the actual thing.

The Illusion of Reality. Every production should create the illusion of reality in the minds of the audience. Even the weirdest fantasy, the most improbable melodrama should seem real at least while they watch it. When they "come to themselves" they may realize that what they have been seeing couldn't possibly have happened, or have happened in just that way, but such a realization should not enter into the emotional response while the play is in progress. Idea, theme, "moral" are for realization when the play is done; the illusion of reality, of watching real people (the griffin in "Alice in Wonderland" as real as any) suffer and rejoice, and complete absorption in the progress of the action on the stage is the fundamental response to gain which the director selects the dramatic values of the play.

The director who works for too great reality as the best means of creating illusion mistakes his aim and the function of his art. But, on the other hand, too great artificiality will have the same effect. If the author and director are to ask the audience to pretend they must do their part. Tawdry scenery, make-shift costumes or insincere or bad acting will destroy illusion. Good acting can overcome poor technical elements since the reactions of the audience are more quickly affected by the animate than the inanimate elements of the production. The imagination of the audience, their ability to pretend, will work more readily with no stimuli than from stimuli that lead in the wrong direction.

Various elements in the audience will demand different degrees of aesthetic distance. The reactions of youth to the same circumstance will be different from those of older people. A child will accept as real what to an older person will be palpably unreal. Both may accept it in the spirit of "let's pretend," but it is the child who cries out to warn the heroine of her danger.

This illusion of reality is easy to create but it is still more easy to lose. Distractions are fatal to it, whether they be distractions connected with the production or aside from it. The former are apt to be the more fatal, because the more fundamental and usually the more lasting. It is hard for an actor, for instance, who is seen for himself, either because he is a great star or because he is personally known to the audience, to lose his own personality entirely and become the character.

Dramatic Values. It has been said that for an audience to be able to enjoy a play they must have "something to root for, something to hate, something to sympathize with and something to laugh at," and Wilkie Collins' advice to playwrights on how to interest the audience was, "Make 'em laugh, make 'em weep, make 'em wait!" The consideration of what elements in his play will arouse the greatest amount of emotional response on the part of his audience is an important one for the director.

Comedy, sympathy, surprise, suspense and "love interest" are certainly among the most frequent and important values used to create response in the audience. Surprise is the weakest of the elements mentioned since it can only be counted on for its full value as long as the play is comparatively new and unknown. It loses much of its effect when the audience may either have read or seen the play before. For the same reason suspense created by anticipation of *what* is going to happen is a less certain and lasting dramatic value than that based on interest in *how* the event is to be brought about. "Love interest" need not, of course, be that of romantic love. Love of God, love of humanity, love of country, and love expressed through other human relationships have for most people an equally sure appeal. Many modern plays show a tendency to deal with other themes than romantic love, though that element has in the past been considered so essential that we sometimes find it "dragged in" where there is no vital connection with the dramatic values of the play. In such a case the director should be careful that it does not serve as a red herring dragged across the trail of the play's true theme.

There are many other values, less common perhaps, but equally powerful in creating audience response. A play that portrays an instance of poetic justice, of "making the punishment fit the crime" appeals to an instinct deep in almost all of us. The Cinderella theme also awakens a response in us. We are all apt to consider ourselves as under-dogs and since we tend to self-association with the people of the play with whom we sympathize, it gives us vicarious satisfaction to see anyone who has been unfortunate come into his own. A sense of familiarity, of seeing things well known to us and of repeating vicariously experiences of our own, will almost certainly arouse emotion in us. In fact, since we have reacted directly to such stimuli before, our responses are apt to be less impersonal in such a case and the director must, especially if the situations shown arouse or could arouse painful responses—which is just as possible in comedy as in any other type of play—be very careful that aesthetic distance is maintained.

Many plays afford more than one set of values but the director must decide on those which he thinks will create the greatest emotional response in his audience. It may be possible to produce the same play for its comedy elements or for the character relationships or story or to emphasize some theme or idea latent in it. Sometimes different acts or scenes in the same play will suggest entirely different values, in which case the director must soften or emphasize them so that they conform to the values he wants to get from the play as a whole. The first act of "Little Eyolf," for example, could be played as almost pure fantasy by putting the emphasis on the unreal symbolic qualities of the Rat-wife scene and the unnatural fascination of the child. The last two acts of the play are psychological drama, necessarily based on a realistic presentation. It is the director's problem therefore to bring out the realistic elements in Act I in order that the last two acts may have their proper value, and the play as a whole be unified.

The dramatic values selected are apt to be slightly different for unknown and well known plays, regardless of their theme or story. An unknown play lends itself to emphasis of those factors that create surprise or suspense, while in a well known classic they cannot be counted on. In the latter the greatest audience response will probably come through enjoyment of the familiar or through novelty of treatment.

Emphasis of Dramatic Values. When the director has determined the dramatic values of the play he must decide on the means to bring them out. This will be largely a matter of emphasis and will depend on the technique with which he handles the various elements of his production. The emphasis and softening of lines, the interpretation of character and character relationships, the picturization of the values of individual scenes and the style and rhythm of the production as a whole will all be governed by the dramatic values the director wishes to present, and will, if correctly used, create in the audience the emotional response that the director as an artist desires for the production which is a work of art.

APPENDICES AND GLOSSARY

PLAY SELECTION

Although the material offered in this and the following Appendices has no immediate connection with the technique used by the director as an interpretive artist, the authors feel that the suggestions it contains may prove helpful to the inexperienced director in his own work with little theatre, community, school or church groups.

A creative artist may conceive a work of art purely to express his own feeling or idea without thought of its effect on anyone else. A writer may even choose to put his creation into dramatic form because that form seems to him to suit the conception best, without thought for its production "on a stage, before an audience." By the very nature of his position as "an agent" or one who stands between, however, the interpretive artist must consider the audience as well as the work of art that he presents to them. To the director the reaction of the audience should be a vital part of his artistic effort and consideration of it should govern his selection of the plays to be presented as well as his method of presenting them.

Community Taste. The director who works in a large community, especially one in which there exists an established "theatre audience," people accustomed to at-

tend and interested in the theatre, may perhaps count on
building an audience from a group having tastes and
ideas similar to his own. For the director in a smaller or
more theatrically isolated community, however, it will
be necessary to gauge carefully the average taste of the
community and to present at least a majority of plays
selected in order to please that taste.

The director who works in such a community over a
period of years can, if he proceeds in the right way,
gradually educate his audience to the point where they
not only accept but enjoy what he considers the finer
things of the theatre. In planning a season of six or
eight plays, he can start by giving one, or perhaps two
that he personally wants to produce because they have
some special interest for him, without consideration of
their so-called box office appeal. If he has chosen the rest
of his program to suit the taste of his community the
one or two plays that do not conform will probably be
accepted without much protest. If, however, he insists on
giving an entire program of plays that are above or
outside the average taste he will soon lose all but a very
small part of his audience.

The director in a small community should be especially careful not to use plays of controversial theme.
Many plays that would pass without question in a large
metropolitan district may arouse feeling in his local community. He should make it a point to know any racial,
religious, political or social shibboleths of the vicinity
and to respect the feeling of his audience with regard
to them.

The plays selected to please the taste of his audience

need never be "trash." With the whole range of dramatic literature to choose from it is possible to find plays that meet that essential requirement and are yet worth while and interesting to do. There are many that will be entertaining and still have educational value either socially or artistically. As a matter of fact, the director can usually count on the educational forces in the community to support at least one classic a season. If the proper approach is made the schools and libraries will be glad to cooperate in making such a production a success. It is usually wise to select one of the better known classics. A Shakespearean play has often surprised and delighted the inexperienced director by proving "a box office hit."

The director need not feel that the presentation of the plays which he selects in order to hold his audience is merely a chore. There will always be a certain satisfaction in presenting them in an appropriate and artistic manner and in emphasizing whatever good points they may have. They will certainly have good points even though they may simply be the power to amuse, or they would not appeal even to the taste of a theatrically uneducated audience.

Budget Restrictions. Unfortunately the director will often find other factors more limiting to his selection of plays than the taste of his audience. Of these the greatest deterrent is apt to be a limited budget. To secure a first class modern play, the group producing it must pay a royalty or rental fee for its use. It is from his royalties that a playwright lives and it is only just that he should receive them. To produce a royalty play without payment of the fee is not only dishonest but subjects the group using it to possibly far greater expense through the processes of the law. Professional play agents have means of checking dramatic productions, even in isolated communities, through their clipping bureaus.

There are, of course, numerous non-royalty plays, but these, except for the classics, are usually not of great artistic worth, although one or two may sometimes be used in a season's program to "balance the budget" or, better, to release money for the royalties on more worth while plays for the rest of the season. To make it acceptable, a non-royalty play will probably require especially careful direction. There are numerous foreign plays well worth doing and old enough not to be covered by the international copyright, but the translations, at least the more recent ones, are apt to be copyrighted. The plays of Ibsen and Oscar Wilde used by many groups as a solution of the royalty problem, present their own difficulties. Wilde's plays are high comedies, the most difficult of all dramatic types for inexperienced actors, since its playing requires a definite acting technique rather than sincerity of characterization. The psychological drama of Ibsen is equally difficult to produce successfully, not from the point of view of untrained actors —here sincerity rather than technique is the most valuable element—but from that of an inexperienced audience. Ibsen is frequently not a "box office draw." In producing the older classics the director will usually find that what he saves on royalty will, unless he has a good store of technical equipment to draw on, be more than offset by what he will have to spend for costumes and the many sets such plays require.

One very interesting way of avoiding the payment of royalties is the production of new and original plays that have neither had a professional production nor been published. There are, however, three drawbacks that the director will encounter. The first and most difficult is that of securing really worth while original scripts that are in adequate shape for production. The second is the fact that when the director has acquired what seems to him a good play, certain weaknesses of structure, characterization, dialogue, etc. will be very apt to show up in rehearsal and the director must be prepared to act as a "play doctor." He must have the knowledge and be able to take the time to help the author correct such faults or his production will not be fair to the play, to author or to audience. A new play should have an extra long rehearsal period and a cast sufficiently experienced not to be thrown out of their characterizations by many changes and much revamping of scenes which have already apparently been set. The third drawback is the lack of advertising that such plays have had. An audience has more interest in a play that they know or have heard something about, whether it be a famous classic or a modern play recently reviewed in the newspapers and magazines. If the author of the new play is from the local community, their knowledge of and interest in him may in some measure offset a lack of other advertising. If in spite of these drawbacks the director can produce even an occasional original play, he is offering true service to the theatre as a whole, for the theatre depends largely upon its playwrights and they, more than any other group, lack opportunity for a hearing in the theatre.

The question of royalty or non-royalty is a nice one for the director. Frequently the interest shown in the production of a much discussed modern play will increase the attendance to where it more than justifies the payment of a high royalty. It is only through an intimate knowledge of his community and its interest that the director can decide such a question and even then his judgment will not always be infallible. What the public will like and be willing to pay for is a question that no one can hope always to answer correctly, but it is one to which the director must give deep and serious consideration, nevertheless.

Technical Limitations. In addition to taste and the budget another factor that must be considered in play selection is the technical facilities at the director's command. In addition to the cost of elaborate sets and costumes, for instance, the director must consider his ability to acquire them either through rental or production.

(If the director has time, facilities and enough interest and ability in his group, making his own sets and costumes, even if they must be simple, will usually prove more satisfactory than renting them. Of course there may be special articles such as unusual pieces of furniture, wigs, boots, etc. that it is impractical to make and impossible to borrow which will have to be rented, but such rentals should be minimized as much as possible. Rental is very apt to be an expense that does not justify itself. The making or borrowing of the needed costumes or props may, on the other hand, be a means of arousing a wider interest in the community.)

Other technical factors to be considered are the size of the stage and auditorium. If the director is working in the "Civic Opera House" he will find it difficult to present intimate psychological plays; if his theatre seats only 250 with a stage proportionally small he will not be wise to attempt a "Cavalcade."

Unless the director is using a professional stage crew, the interest that exists or that he can arouse in "back stage work" will have some influence on his selection of plays. Plays of many scene changes should not be attempted unless the director can greatly simplify them or make adequate preparation, including rehearsal, to handle them quickly. Many an otherwise fine production has failed because the audience was made to sit through many long intermissions.

Casting Considerations. The question of casting is necessarily of the utmost importance in connection with play selection and should be given most careful consideration. The subject of casting will be given more detailed consideration in Appendix B. In this connection, however, the director should be sure that he has actors capable of adequately interpreting the most important roles—not necessarily the longest, but those most vital to the play values—before definitely deciding on the play. In working with inexperienced players, however, the director should base such a decision on his judgment of the actor's possibilities, that is, the point to which he may develop if working along the lines of characterization needed by the particular play, rather than his general ability.

Play Cutting. The right of the director to cut or rearrange a play in order to make it conform to certain requirements is one for careful consideration. It is usually permissible to cut a play in order that certain undesirable elements not essential to the play's values may be eliminated, to solve technical difficulties of production or to make an old play conform to modern requirements.

Under the first head will fall such details as the elimination of profanity or other elements likely to prove offensive to the audience. If they are allowed to remain the shock that they give to the audience may be great enough to destroy aesthetic distance and produce too direct and personal reactions. In such a case cutting is not only permissible but necessary.

The solution of technical difficulties, other than that of reducing a very long play to acceptable time limits, is usually attained through rearrangement rather than cutting. Unimportant scenes, needing or calling for a special setting, can and often are omitted in the production of classic plays, but care must be taken not to eliminate any scene no matter how apparently short and unimportant that contains plot material. Minor incidents that require certain technical effects or speeches that allude to them may be cut if it is technically impossible for the director to reproduce the effects. The same is true from the standpoint of acting. It is better to eliminate or change lines that refer to laughter on the part of a certain character if the actor playing that part, and otherwise satisfactory, is unable to acquire a natural stage laugh. Again care must be used that the elements eliminated are not in any way essential to the plot or dramatic values.

Casting difficulties owing to too small an acting group and a large cast may sometimes be solved by the elimination of unimportant characters and the distribution of their lines among other characters. Sometimes it is also possible to fuse two characters into one. In the first instance the lines must be carefully apportioned so that they will be in character for the person to whom they are given. In the second case care must be taken that the characters fused do not have conflicting characteristics or those impossible to reconcile in one individual.

Obsolete words and phrases found in plays of a long past period or stilted and unnatural expressions in those of the more immediate past are better cut. The audience either fails to understand them or reacts to them in a manner not intended by the author. It is sometimes necessary for the director to substitute a more modern phrasing for the speeches cut.

Even where cutting for any of the above reasons is permissible it is better for the director to secure the effect he wants through a shift of emphasis if such is possible. When, however, he does cut the play, the director must be careful of two things, first to keep the story clear by preservation of the plot continuity and second to preserve the correct proportions of the play by keeping his climaxes relative. The elimination of a scene or part of a scene may bring two low scenes or two climaxes into too close relation.

Variety. In addition to solving all his other problems of play selection the director must plan for variety in his program of plays. This is advisable from the viewpoints of both production and of audience reaction. Even though his audience may show a marked preference for some type of play, they will soon tire of it if they are given nothing else. Moreover a schedule of plays of the same type will soon exhaust the players available for the kind of roles required. Settings and properties are apt to be of the same genre and this makes the attainment of variety in production difficult.

The following is suggested as a practical program for a season of six productions.

1. Character comedy.
2. Folk drama or fantasy.
3. Society comedy.
4. Classic or play of social significance.
5. Mystery or story play.
6. Character or society comedy.

CASTING

The question of casting will be vitally influenced by the director's fundamental purpose in his work. If his aim is to produce as fine and finished productions as are possible, his policy in casting will undoubtedly be to use the best actor for each part available. He will choose his casts for their ability and will put aside as largely as possible all other considerations. If, on the other hand, his object is to conduct a theatre that will serve the citizens of the community by giving them an opportunity for acquiring the cultural advantages supplied by work in the theatre and for self-expression, he will use as large a group as is available and will try to see that all who so desire are given a chance to act and if he does not entirely disregard their ability, that at least cannot be his sole consideration.

The work of most directors will not fall sharply and decidedly into either of these groups perhaps. Every director should be enough for an artist to wish his productions to be worth while from the artistic point of view even when his main purpose in making them is to fill a social community need. On the other hand no director, unless he is working in the professional theatre, can entirely disregard the community interest in his productions. His audience must be drawn from the community and the larger his group of actors the wider the personal interest in his theatrical enterprise. The director whose aim is the best possible production must be always on the look-out for new material both for the sake of variety in casting and to keep his group from stagnating. The director whose purpose is to afford the community self-expression must yet manage to attain a certain artistic worth in his productions, for no community is altruistic enough long to support a theatre that gives only mediocre performances, no matter how worthy its purpose. The two policies may be fused to a certain extent, especially if the director works in the same community and with the same organization over a period of years, but the director must maintain a casting policy that will further his primary purpose. We may assume, however, that no matter what his policy is he will cast his productions as adequately as circumstances allow. In order to do so he must give the following facts much consideration.

Acting Ability. Acting ability will be found to rest mainly on the amount of imagination the actor possesses and only secondarily on the technique he has been able to acquire. Technical perfection if it is not based upon imagination will at best result in a facile but shallow characterization. Fortunately it is usually imagination that inspires in the non-professional a desire to act. The director, moreover, can soon teach the imaginative actor a technique that will assure a fairly easy performance.

Granted therefore that he has a group imaginatively alive from which to cast his play the director will choose actors for the individual roles on the basis of physical appearance, voice and personality.

Physical Appearance. This is the least vital of the three elements in most cases, for the audience has as a rule no preconceived idea of what the character will look like. There are of course certain characters in well known plays who through tradition are expected to be of a certain type. Any audience might be excused for resenting a Malvolio who was short and fat. Only in such a case, or when the physical appearance of the character is a vital element either in the plot or in obtaining the desired dramatic values, must the director be limited by it in his casting. Make-up and the actor's bearing can do much to supply the desired physical appearance.

Voice. The actor's voice is a factor that needs much more serious consideration. Its range and flexibility and the actor's ability to use it will be found to mean much not alone to characterization but to the dramatic values of the play. It should be suitable not only to the character but to the type of lines he has to speak.

The director should try to choose actors whose voices are pleasant in quality and have variety of tone for long roles. Even though it may be quite in keeping for the character to speak in a gruff, disagreeable voice or a monotonous tone, such qualities will become tiresome to the audience who must listen to them extensively through an entire production.

On the other hand, a very beautiful and flexible voice, used simply for these qualities will become equally tiresome. Many actors with fine speaking voices and trained in the arts of speech use them simply as lovely instruments. It is the imaginative emotional quality behind the voice that keeps it vital and interesting.

Personality. It is very difficult to judge the personality of an unknown actor from his individual personality, for the projection necessary to carry it across the footlights often has some strange power of changing it. A woman who is very attractive and charming off stage may lose those qualities and some quiet and mouselike little creature may appear brilliant and scintillating when seen on the stage. It is an actor's stage personality then that the director must consider when casting.

Stage personality must be judged by the actor's effect on an audience. The director who wants a certain character to have a definite effect upon the audience must cast in the role an actor whose stage personality is apt to produce that effect. Various elements in the audience will react differently to the same character. They will also react differently to an actor. The director who gives thought to such reactions can often use this factor of personality to unify the reaction of the audience. For instance the director decides that the women in the audience are pretty sure to like and sympathize with the hero of the play, but he does not feel equally sure of the men. He has two actors either of whom he thinks might play the role well. Of the two men, however, one is always very much liked by the men in the audience. If he casts that particular actor in the part it is probable that he will have sympathy for the hero from his entire audience.

An actor's personality can often be used advantageously to help secure definite dramatic value. If there is a character in the play that is written unsympathetically but which the director wishes to present sympathetically because he believes that such a presentation will greatly intensify the emotional reaction of his audience, he must count on the sympathetic personality of the actor to help him do it. On the other hand the use of an actor whose personality is sympathetic, no matter how well he may interpret the character, in a part that it is desirable to have the audience dislike may have the effect of distorting the play values.

Type Casting. The director working with untrained actors must, of necessity, do much type casting. For his own sake, however, and in order to develop as flexible a group as possible he will avoid it whenever he can. He must study his actors closely and when he finds one who shows imagination and some facility, he should begin to try him out in parts as varied as possible. In this way he will develop an actor of much greater value to the group. Not only can he be called upon for parts that it is not easy to type cast, but he can be used more frequently in varied parts than he could be if he were always cast to one particular type of character.

One thing that the director must beware of is the assumption that an untried actor can play a particular type because he *is* that type. Often the type that an actor plays best is in direct contrast to his own character. We can all see the characteristics of other people more clearly than our own. Often, too, the actor enjoys more the creation of a role foreign to his own character; it gives him a greater sense of freedom and release from his own everyday existence.

Try-outs. If the director is not well acquainted with his acting group some form of preliminary try-out will probably be necessary. Even if he does not try-out for the entire cast he will probably want to have certain of the roles read by more than one actor before he makes any definite decision as to casting them. In any event the holding of try-outs is desirable for two reasons; it promotes a feeling of fair-play in the group and it often brings new talent to the director's attention which he may use later if not in the actual play being read. Try-outs must be conducted in a thoroughly matter of fact and impersonal manner or they may do more harm than good. The director should thank all who read; in many instances he can offer explanations to those who are rejected that will prevent any feeling of disparagement on their part. Such explanations as that the actor's voice is too similar in quality to other voices in the cast, that he is not tall enough or he is too tall to play opposite another member in the cast, that his personality is too sympathetic for the role, etc. will be accepted by the candidate without question.

The director should not expect too much from preliminary readings, especially if the group is unfamiliar with the play. He can, however, usually get a fairly accurate idea of the personal appearance, voice quality and personality of the actor. He will probably not learn much of the player's ability. Many people who give poor and rather wooden sight readings develop remarkably when they have a chance really to work on the part. On the other hand it is not unusual to find actors whose sight reading is easy and flexible, but who develop very little in the course of rehearsal. The director must of course learn to discount the nervousness and self-consciousness which afflict even fairly experienced actors at a try-out.

Ensemble Playing. Unless he is working with a very large acting group so that the personnel of the casts in his productions is different each time, the director will soon find that there is developing among certain of his actors a feeling for ensemble playing. He should do all in his power to encourage it. It is only when all the members of a cast play together and cooperate that we get a finished production. It is an element that is difficult to teach, but that will come naturally as the players get used to the various methods used by one another.

In this connection, the director should consider his cast as a whole when selecting its individual members. If he knows that two actors play together well, he may make a point of using them in the same cast whenever possible, though for variety's sake he will avoid casting them in parts that have the same relationship. In one play they may be brother and sister, in another lovers, in a third father and daughter—the character relationship will not affect their responsiveness to each other as actors. It is even more important of course, if the director has two players who clash, not to use them in the same production. Sometimes the director will find that he has an actor—often a really good actor—who is always a center of disturbance in every cast in which he appears. Such an individual not only destroys all ensemble playing, but if not dealt with promptly and severely may disrupt the morale of the group. It is always better to sacrifice the finest actor than to entertain such a disturbing influence.

Extraneous Problems. As in the matter of play selection the director is apt to have pressure brought to bear on him to lead him to cast for other than artistic reasons. In the case of casting such pressure should be resisted, and only given way to in extreme cases. Even when he does give way the director should try to prevent its being apparent that he does so. If the director feels that it is absolutely necessary for him to use the daughter of the president of the organization in order that the president may give the theatre the new floor cloth which it needs so badly, let him choose a play that has a role for her which will not tax her ability too far, and announce that he has selected that particular play because it will give her unusual talents an opportunity. In other words let the initiative apparently come from the director, rather than have the group realize that he has been forced to use an actress of whose ability he has a low opinion. The director should stand as firmly upon his artistic prerogatives in casting as in any other phases of producing or else the artistic integrity of his work will most certainly suffer.

Distribution of Actors. The director who has a limited amount of good acting material available should "budget" his actors over his whole season. If he uses too many of his best people in one production, either his other plays will fall below the standard level of acting or else he will run into danger of having to use the same people too frequently. Only very rarely do the audience enjoy seeing the same actors over and over again. It is a temptation which the director must resist to use competent people in all roles even at the expense of monotony in casting.

If, however, he will be content with expert actors in

the three or four most important roles, the use of less expert actors to fill out the cast will not only broaden the interest in the group, but will give him a chance to discover new talent and to develop it to the point of competence. An "all-star" production may be desirable occasionally as a special attraction, but the proper distribution of available acting material over the entire season, so that the better actor is not over-worked and that no production suffers from inadequate casting, is one of the important casting problems that the director must solve.

REHEARSALS

Rehearsals should be conducted in a thoroughly business-like manner. The director should encourage a friendly, social feeling among the cast, but it must not be allowed to interfere with the business in hand. The actors derive enjoyment from their work and will feel better repaid if they are kept pretty strictly to it. During an evening's rehearsal the director may allow two or three recesses of perhaps ten minutes each. Such intermissions allow the actors to become better acquainted with each other personally and this promotes a feeling of ease among them which is beneficial to ensemble playing. They also provide a chance for relaxation and rest, necessary to people whose work is based primarily on expended energy and who have not the technique necessary to enable them to save themselves while at work.

Promptness. One of the most vital elements in a business-like rehearsal is to start it promptly at the hour called. If the director has consulted the convenience of his cast before calling the rehearsal there should be no excuse for tardiness. If any actor is detained for a good reason he should notify the director and let him know definitely when to expect him. The director can then start promptly working on a scene in which that actor is not involved. Some people are habitually tardy through carelessness and such tardiness if permitted will arouse a feeling of resentment in those who make the effort to get to rehearsal on time. There is nothing so injurious to the morale of production as to allow any member of the cast to feel that he is wasting time. If an actor is not needed during the early part of the evening's work, he may be excused from it and a later hour appointed by the director for his arrival.

The director's own promptness at rehearsal should go without saying. He cannot naturally expect promptness from his cast unless he is meticulous in observing the appointed hour himself.

Number of Rehearsals. The number of rehearsals for a finished production will depend on the difficulty of the play, and sometimes on its length, and on the size and ability of the cast. The arrangement of rehearsals of the various parts will also vary with the type of play, with the number of acts and their respective difficulty, and with the number of people involved in each. If the director is working with a fairly experienced cast, it will not be necessary to devote as much time to the preliminary work and he can, if the play requires it, spend more time on interpretation and polishing or shorten his rehearsal period.

The amount of time allowed for rehearsing a production must be decided on the basis of how many rehearsals the director thinks will be necessary and the frequency with which he can get his cast together. After the preliminary work is done, business and movements set, etc., it is often well to call the next few rehearsals at longer intervals in order to allow time for memorization. The

intervals should not be long enough, however, to allow
the business and movement to become hazy in the actor's
mind. Four rehearsals a week, on Monday, Tuesday,
Thursday and Friday, frequently proves satisfactory except for the period just mentioned when the number can
be dropped to two or three. Just before production, also,
the director may find it desirable to hold rehearsals more
frequently.

Before the play goes into rehearsal a definite date
should be set for production. If the date of production
is allowed to be contingent on rehearsal progress there is
almost certain to be a relaxation of effort on the part of
the cast and sometimes on that of the director as well.
The having to be ready by a definite time will be found to
be a decided spur to effort. For much the same reason a
too long rehearsal period is undesirable. Even when it
does not relax the effort it is apt to cause the actors to
become stale. The play and their roles lose interest for
them and even though the excitement of dress-rehearsals
and production may renew their interest something of
the staleness is apt to show in their work.

The length of the individual rehearsal period will depend on what element in the play the director is working
for at the time. Actors can stand a longer rehearsal when
they are receiving purely technical instruction than after
they have begun to work on characterization. The average length should not be much over three hours. When
the cast are obviously tired out it is well for the director
to stop work. An inexperienced actor has no technique to
fall back on and when fatigue has sapped his energy there

is not usually much left. If the director feels that he cannot dismiss the rehearsal he can perhaps switch to the perfecting of purely technical details which require much less energy on the part of the cast. If the rehearsal is held too long and the actor pushed too hard he is apt to develop a feeling of futility, lack of interest and discouragement which counteracts any possible gain he may receive from further work.

Rehearsal Schedule. Before starting on a regular schedule of rehearsals it is desirable for the director to hold several general readings at which parts are given out but no attempt is made to plan business. They are devoted to any discussions of characterizations or character relationships that may arise and to settling any questions of the meaning or proper reading of lines. The whole play should be covered at each of these readings. The number necessary will depend on the type of play and the imaginative ability of the cast. Following these general readings, some such schedule as that appended will probably prove satisfactory for the average three act play with a cast of average ability. Less time needs to be spent on Acts II and III since the actors will have learned much of the general technique of movement and business during the rehearsals of Act I. Characterizations will also have been pretty much established during the first rehearsals.

> I Entire Play. Playing areas and positions, movement and business may be roughly indicated, but in sufficient detail to be sure that the floor plans and various features of the set will be adequate

for the effects the director hopes to get. If anything appears to be inadequate or wrong it should be changed before the next rehearsal.

   II Entire Play. Check all business planned at previous rehearsal and smooth out any hitches. These two rehearsals and the general readings should give the actors a pretty accurate idea of the play as a whole.

  III Act I twice. Detailed work on business and line readings. Act II once. Check business from previous rehearsals and add details.

  IV Act I three times without scripts. Work on lines and cues and do not bother with business unless it is very wrong.

   V Act II Detailed work.

  VI Act I once.
       Act II twice. Checking business.

 VII Act I once.
       Act II once.
       Act III Preliminary work.

VIII Act I three times without scripts.

  IX Act III Detailed work.

   X Act I once.
       Act II twice without scripts.

  XI Act III three times without scripts. Check business.

 XII All Acts. Intensive work on special scenes.

XIII Entire play. Work for smoothness and finish.

XIV Entire play. Tempo and cueing.

 XV Entire play without interruption for flow. Time each act and if the play or any part of it seems to be running too long make any necessary cuts before the next rehearsal.

XVI Line Rehearsal. Check any special readings. Watch emphasis and clarity. Make and work over any necessary cuts. This rehearsal need not be held on the stage. This will leave the stage free for a crew rehearsal if the Stage Manager is competent to conduct it.

XVII Prop Rehearsal. It is better if all properties can be assembled for this rehearsal. Certainly all that are vital to business should be available, chairs, etc. All hand props without fail.

XVIII Dress Rehearsal. This should be taken quietly. The director should not worry about character interpretation. The actors will probably be distracted by costumes and settings and the director should concentrate on technical details.

XIX Dress Rehearsal. The director should feel free to interrupt if it seems absolutely necessary but the interruptions should be as few as possible. It is often advisable to wait until the end of each act and then go back over any parts that need correction.

XX Dress Rehearsal. Conduct this rehearsal as though it were a performance. A short "pep talk" at the close with expression of appreciation for the actors' work and the play is ready for production.

Memorizing Lines. Individuals memorize in such various ways and at such different speeds that the director should not be too arbitrary about the learning of lines. It is usually wiser not to encourage the inexperienced player to start learning them before the parts have been analyzed and characterizations and character relationship thoroughly understood. Otherwise wrong inflections and readings are acquired which it is hard to correct. Memorizing lines is also easier for most people if they associate the line with the movement and business that is to accompany it.

One very good rule is to require every member of the

cast to know all his lines so that there will be at least eight rehearsals at which every one is letter perfect. Actors, like other people, procrastinate and most of them dislike memorization, so that the director must make it his own responsibility to see that lines are learned sufficiently ahead of production to allow for the necessary polishing and finishing of the production.

DIRECTOR'S AND ACTOR'S GLOSSARY

Above: Farther up stage.

Action: The progress of the story as expressed through movement, business and dialogue.

Action, physical: Movement and business.

Ad Lib: (Ad libitum—at pleasure) Lines or business not supplied or specified by the script.

Arc Cross: See curved cross.

Area, arbitrary: A section of the stage having an attention-value relative to the rest of the playing space.

Area, playing: A part of the stage or a piece or group of furniture used for playing an individual scene, as distinct from the stage as a whole.

Asides: Speeches not addressed to the other characters on the stage. They may be spoken as vocalized thought or addressed directly to the audience, depending on the type of production.

Attitude: A significant and expressive position of the body or part of it.

Back Stage: Behind the scenes. Sometimes used to include Green Room and Dressing Rooms.

Bearing: The use of the actor's body to indicate character.

Below: Farther down stage.

Breaking Up: The changing of the stage picture by the use of movement and business.

Build: To increase the tension throughout a speech or a scene of action up to the climax.

Business: Detailed pantomimic action. The term is sometimes used to cover movement as well.

Business, imposed: Business invented by the actor, director or playwright for purposes other than telling the story.

Business, necessary: The business demanded by the story.

Carry: To be effectively audible or visible to the audience.

Center Stage: The middle of the stage, usually gauged from side to side.

Character parts: Roles dependent more on individual characteristics than on emotional values.

Characterize: To create a vivid and individual character.

Characterization, objective: To create a character through portrayal of his outward manifestations.

Characterization, subjective: To create a character by portrayal of his thoughts and emotions.

Clarity: A clear presentation of action and story. When applied to speech, distinct enunciation.

Climax: The point of greatest tension in an individual scene or in the play as a whole.

Counter: To make a secondary movement in the opposite direction to a primary movement either to balance the stage picture or to remain uncovered.

Counter Focus: A focus away from the center of interest, or in a large group, a focus on one of the lesser characters in the group.

Cover: To stand in front of an actor or piece of business so as to hide him or it from the audience. When done intentionally it is usually called masking.

Cross: To move in any direction. (A cross is usually indicated in the prompt script by an X)

Cue: The last two or three words of the preceding speech which an actor learns in order to know when to speak, to move, or to perform some piece of business.

Dialogue: The lines spoken by the actors.

Down Stage: The part of the stage closest to the audience.

Dramatic values: Those elements in an individual scene or in the play as a whole that arouse emotional response from the audience.

Dress Stage: To keep the stage picture balanced, usually by a counter movement and maintained focus.

Dress the set: To supply and arrange the details necessary for the completion of the setting.

Emphasis: The intensification of any element in the production in order to bring it to the attention of the audience.

Entrance: To come on stage. The doorway or opening in the set through which the actors come and go.

Exit: To leave the stage.

Exit Line: The last line an actor speaks before he leaves the stage.

Exposition: The playwright's presentation of antecedent material necessary for the audience to know in order to understand the play.

Expository Scenes: Scenes of exposition.

Extras: Characters having no lines and usually not necessary to the story of the play. They are never prominent in it as individuals.

Feeder Line: A speech in comedy that supplies the point to the line that actually gets the laugh.

Focus: The center of interest in the scene toward which the other actors turn.

Foreshadow: To indicate by business or speech something important that will happen later.

Gesture: A motion usually of the hands, arms or head, in response to a transitory stimulus.

Give: To move slightly back or away to avoid contact with another actor who approaches directly or crosses in front. Usually only a matter of a short step.

Given Scene: A scene in which one actor has the most important business or lines and is permitted by the director to take the stage.

Hold: To drop all speech and action during laughter or applause. A hold, as distinct from a planned pause, for any other reason is usually accidental and always undesirable.

Illusion of Reality: The acceptance by the audience of the setting, characters and story as a real place with real people undergoing actual experience.

Level: 1. A platform, steps or ramp that raises the playing space above the level of the stage.

2. An imaginary line drawn across the stage at any distance from the curtain line but parallel to it.

Mask: To cover or hide a piece of business from the audience.

Motivate: To supply a dramatic reason for a speech or action other than its technical purpose.

Move Back: To step directly back from the position in which the actor is standing.

Move Down: To move directly down stage, at the same distance from the center of the stage.

Move Forward: To move in the direction the actor is facing.

Move In: To move toward the center of the stage on the same level.

Move Out: To move toward the side of the stage on the same level.

Move Up: To move toward the back of the stage at the same distance from stage center.

Movement: A change of bodily position on the stage such as crossing, rising, sitting, etc.

Movement, imposed: Movement supplied for technical purposes or for reasons other than telling the story.

Movement, inherent: Movement necessary to the story of the play.

Movement of the play: The story of the play as shown through physical movement, dialogue, stage pictures, etc. (See Action)

Open Up: To turn or play more directly to the audience. Sometimes, when addressed to a group of actors, it may mean to move farther apart.

Over Lap: To start a speech before the preceding one is quite finished.

Over Play: To exaggerate unduly either business or speech.

Pacing Scene: A scene during which one of the characters walks about the stage continuously.

Picking Up Cues: The following of a cue by the next speech. The important consideration is the interval between.

Places: The term used by the director and stage manager in summoning actors to be ready for the opening of a scene during either rehearsal or production.

Play In: To play toward the center of the stage.

Play on a level: To play at the same distance from the curtain line.

Play Out: Play toward the audience.

Plot Lines: Lines that forward the story of the play. They include lines that tell necessary facts that have preceded the play's opening.

Plugging: Giving an exaggerated and unneeded emphasis.

Point: To emphasize.

Production: All the elements involved in putting a play on the stage taken as a whole. Also the time during which the play runs.

Proscenium: The arch or picture frame that surrounds the stage.

Project: To throw the voice out so that it carries into the auditorium effectively.

Prompt: To give an actor his lines when his memory fails.

Prompt Script: The copy of the play kept by the director or stage manager, in which all business and other information necessary to the production are recorded.

Properties: The furniture and small objects used by the actors in the course of production. Commonly known as "props." Furniture and other large objects are known as stage props while the smaller objects are hand props. Personal props are hand props belonging to and usually used by only one character.

Rhythm: Recurring emphasis. (See Text)

Routine: A series of actions carefully planned and rehearsed.

Scene: Speech and action involving one set of characters. The beginning and end of scenes are usually marked by entrances or exits. No change of place is necessary. The term is used in another sense to indicate the locale of the action.

Set: To rehearse movement or business until it is thoroughly established. Also used as an abbreviation of setting.

Setting: The place in which the action occurs.

Shared Scene: A scene in which two actors are of equal importance and in which they are given equally advantageous positions on the stage.

Sides: Typed copies of the actor's role giving only his own cues and speeches. They usually consist of pages half the size of an ordinary sheet of typewriting paper, for convenience of handling.

Soften: To under emphasize a speech or piece of business.

Soliloquy: A speech, usually longer than an aside, spoken by an actor alone on the stage. It presents audibly the character's supposed thought.

Stage: The space reserved for the action of the play, usually a platform.

Stage Picture: The setting and arrangement of characters on the stage.

Stage Turn: To turn with the face to the audience.

Static Scene: A scene of conversation with little or no action.

Steal: To play a little away from the other actor without its being apparent to the audience, in order to open up.

Straight Part: A role that depends on emotional values rather than individual characteristics.

Strong: Forceful; having the power to attract attention.

Style: The mode and manner of presentation.

Take Stage: To be or go up stage of the other characters.

Technical Purpose: A reason for movement or business other than those involved in the characters or story.

Telescoping: The speaking of their lines simultaneously by two or more actors.

Tempo: The rate of playing.

Throw away: To soften or under emphasize a line.

Time: To plan business or movement and speech so that they correlate correctly.

Topping: The beginning of a speech with greater intensity or at a higher pitch than the preceding one ended.

Trim: Furniture added to a stage setting in order to keep it from seeming bare but not used in the course of the action.

Turn Back: To make a turn with the face away from the audience.

Turn In: To turn more toward the center of the stage.

Turn Out: To turn toward the side of the stage. Sometimes to turn more toward the audience.

Uncover: To move out from behind another actor or a piece of furniture in order to be clearly visible to the audience.

Up Stage: The part of the stage farthest from the audience.

Values: (See Dramatic Values)

Weak: Lacking in force; with little attention value.

INDEX

A